Unknown
Rumi

Other Works by Nevit O. Ergin

Crazy As We Are
The Dîvân-i Kebîr of Mevlana Jalaluddin Rumi
(English Translation in 22 Volumes)
A Rose Garden
Divine Wine
The Glory of Absence
Magnificent One
Forbidden Rumi
Tales of a Modern Sufi
The Rubâîler of Rumi
The Sufi Path of Annihilation

Unknown
Rumi

Selected Rubais of
Mevlana Jalaluddin Rumi
and Commentary by

Nevit O. Ergin

Powerhouse Publishing
Los Angeles, California

Printed in the United States of America

ISBN: 978-0-9646348-5-5 (paperback)
ISBN: 978-0-9646348-6-2 (hardcover)
ISBN: 978-0-9646348-7-9 (e-book)

Library of Congress Control Number: 2015935337

Available from Amazon.com and other retail outlets.
Available on Kindle and other devices.

This book was typeset in Minion Pro with Ondine as display typeface.

Pꟼ
Powerhouse Publishing
4223 Verdugo View Drive
Los Angeles, California 90065
USA
www.ReadingRumi.com

Introduction

We are the statutes of perception. Our mother and father are perceptions, and we are the children of perception. There are an infinite number of levels of perception before and after humanity. Our human level is just a glimpse of it: Perception comes from the infinite and goes to the infinite.

Perception is divided into two kinds: Dualistic and non-dualistic. Mevlana mastered both of them.

Ninety-nine percent of humanity has dualistic perception. In dualistic perception, we look at each other as predator and prey. We see good and evil. We think in terms of you and me. We get tangled up in the institutions of faith and reason.

Non-dualistic perception is Nothingness, Absence, total annihilation of the self. In the Eastern traditions, it is called Advaita. In one of his longer poems [gazels] Mevlana describes it as follows:

> I saw Absence in my dream last night.
> I was amazed by His beauty. I became bewildered.
>
> I was out of myself until early dawn
> Because of the beauty, maturity
> And kindness of Absence.
>
> I compared Absence to a ruby mine.
> I dressed in a satin of its color.
>
> I heard the sound of lovers.
> I listened to their voices saying,
> "May it do you good."
>
> I saw a circle
> That had become drunk with Absence.
> Then, I saw that ring
> Like an earring on my ear.

I saw a form in the light of Absence.
I saw the Soul of souls on his face.

When I saw the rough sea,
My soul became exalted
With a hundred kinds of excitement.

Hundreds of thousands of screams and yells
Came from the sky.
I would become a slave, a servant
To such a messenger.[1]

It's no wonder that so many people do not understand Mevlana. To see this way, non-dualistic perception must be experienced.

To reach non-dualistic perception requires total annihilation of self. A person's gender, age, or profession don't matter; without total annihilation, they will not reach non-dualistic perception.

To reach non-dualistic perception, a person has to go on a long, hard climb up a very steep mountain. They must reach the summit to understand, to see what Mevlana sees.

Unfortunately, most humans don't get past the base of this mountain. They are too world hungry, too satisfied with what they find in this world.

For this collection, we have chosen rubais that reflect both types of perception. There are many, many rubais that reflect the summit and, we urge you to read these most carefully.

Mevlana not only climbed the mountain;
Mevlana is the mountain.
May Mevlana be known.

Nevit O. Ergin
San Mateo, CA

Special Thanks

to Meral Ekmekçioğlu, Mahmoud Ghanadan,
Kavous Barghi, Zafer Gezgin, Edmond
Gorginian, the scholars at Stanford University,
Ishan Vest, and Millicent Alexander
for their support and participation
throughout this project.

Absence is Essence; everything else is an attribute.
Absence is health; everything else is an illness.
This world is a big headache, a grand illusion.
Absence is the real treasure in the world.[2]

-Mevlana Jalaluddin Rumi

This world is nothing more than a magnificent lie. A person who annihilates their "self" sees that.

-Nevit O. Ergin

The Rubais
and
Commentary

Religion is something for humans before they reach fanâ [annihilation]. After reaching fanâ, there is no Islam, no Christianity, nor any other religion.

1.

عاشق تو یقین دان که مسلمان نبود
در مذهب عشق کفر و ایمان نبود
در عشق تن و عقل و دل و جان نبود
هر کس که چنین نکست او آن نبود

Know this very well: a lover cannot be a Muslim.
In the religion of Love, there is no faith, no blasphemy;
Neither body nor soul, neither reason nor heart.
Whoever is not like that is not a lover.

Şunu iyice bil ki: Âşık Müslüman olamaz.
Âşk mezhebinde imana ve küfüre yer yoktur.
Ne beden vardır, ne akıl, ne can vardır, ne de gönül.
Kim böyle değilse o Âşık değildir.

This path is paved with cobblestones of fire. Annihilation [fanâ] is the fire. However, when one annihilates their self, when one dies before their death, they discover the biggest paradise. They see. They understand.

2.

اوّل بهزار لطف بنواخــــت مرا

آ خربهزار غصّه بگذاخــت مرا

جون مُهره مهره خویسرے باختــرا

جون مَن اوشدم بِنداخــت مرا

First, He pampered me with a thousand favors,
Then burned me with a thousand troubles.
He was playing with me, like a dice of His Love.
When I died to myself and became Him,
He threw me out.

Önce beni binlerce iltifâtla okşadı.
Sonra binlerce dertle yaktı.
Benimle âşkının zarı gibi oynuyordu.
Ben, kendimde ölüp O olduğumda, fırlattı attı beni.

The one who stays with the world is the one who struggles through with heart, soul, body. Only the one who escapes from existence to reach Essence sees that. This is the adventure, the traveling we do. It takes a long time, but anybody who doesn't start this journey stays forever stuck on a page of literature.

3.

ناكى باشى ذدوردنظاره مـا

ماجاره كريم وعشق بعاره مـا

جان كيست كمينه طفل هُوارهٔ مـا

دل كيست يكى عزيب آواره مـا

How long will you look at us
From a distance?
We dressed the wounds.
Love is our poor friend.
Who is soul? A helpless baby in our cradle.
Who is heart? Our strange guest.

Ne kadar zaman bize uzaktan bakacaksın?
Dertlere deva biziz.
Aşk, bizim bir yoksul dostumuz.
Ruh kimdir? Beşikteki çaresiz bebek.
Gönül kimdir? Bizim garip misafirimiz.

At one stage of annihilation of the self, exuberance, Love comes. This Love is a result of annihilation. Any other love is simply symbolic love. Until one finds Love, Love keeps telling us to get busy, to fast, do breathing, finish our transformation.

4.

خزعشق نبودهيچ دسار سرا
بى اول و بى آخر و آ غاز مرا
جان مى دهذار درونه آواز مرا
كاى كاهل راه عشق دربازمرا

I don't have a friend besides Love.
Love was with me before I came into this world
And it is still with me.
Soul yells, "O lazy one on Love's way,
Come on, hurry up, reach me."

Aşktan başka arkadaşım yok.
Ben bu dünyaya gelmeden önce de âşk benleydi
Ve hâlâ benimle.
"Ey aşkın yolunda ki tembel, acele et,
Bana ulaş" diye canım bana sesleniyor.

Our mind is the world of relativity, the world of dual concepts like good and bad, death and life, God and creatures. In other words, of dualistic perception. While we are in our mind, we experience so many problems. Once we annihilate our self, all of the differences merge; there is no perceiver, no perceived; we reach safety and peace. This is non-dualistic perception.

5.

عاشق همه سال مست ورسوا باذا
دیوانه وسورین وسیدا باذا
باهُشیاری غصه هرجین خوریم
جون مست بلذیم هرجه باذا باذا

**The lover should be crazy-insane,
Scorned, disgraced, and drunk all year long.
We are susceptible to suffering when we are awake,
But when we are drunk, everything is good.**

Aşık, bütün yıl deli-divane, rezil-rüsva
Ve sarhoş olmalıdır.
Ayıkken dertlere düşeriz de sarhoşken
Her şey ne âlâ.

During the journey of annihilation of self, sometimes we feel like we're in control of everything, other times that we're nothing. After total annihilation [*fanâ*], we see nothing around us. We see that this world doesn't exist, that we're not here, that this is our shadow.

6.

كه مى‌كفتم كه من اسيرم خود را
كه بغزه زنان كه من اسيرم خود را
اَن دفتا ازين بس بندیرم خود را
بكرفتم اين كه من نكيرم خود را

I used to say, "I am the master of myself."
Sometimes I was a slave.
Those times have gone.
Now I am not my self.
Now I am beyond my self.

"Ben geçmişte kendimin hem esiriydim,
Hem ustasıydım" derdim.
O devirler çoktan geçti ve ben şimdi kendim değilim.
Kendimden ötedeyim.

Mevlana is referring to being in the middle of the journey of annihilation of self, the middle of this great mountain. He is giving up his soul and body. At the summit of the mountain, there is no soul, no body, no creation, nothing.

7.

ما اَطْيَبَ ما اللَّ ما اَجَـلَّنا
كَتَامًهَا وَلَمْ تَكَنَّ ابْدَانًا
اِنْ شَاءَ بِنَا كَرَامَةً مَوْلًا نَا
يَغْفُو وَيُعِيدُ نَا كَما اَبْدَانَا

I was heart and soul without a body before,
Pure, clean, pleasant.
My master built my body as a guest house;
He placed the soul in it.
If You are so kind, do me a favor: Pardon me.
Recreate me as You did before;
Bring me back to life.

Biz bedenleri olmayan gönüller ve ruhlardık.
Saf, temiz ve latiftik.
Yaratanımız, bedenlerimizi bir misafir evi
Gibi kullanmamız için yarattı ve
Ruhlarımızı içine koydu.
Lütuf ederse, bağışlar bizi. Nasıl önceden
Yarattıysa, gene yaratır, tekrar diriltir bizi.

Mevlana again refers to being in the middle of the journey of annihilation of self; he is still aware of his existence.One must go beyond existence to experience non-existence.

8.

First I learned about myself by imitating others.
Although I was aware of my existence,
I did not comprehend my being.
Because I didn't see, I didn't recognize myself,
I was only hearing my name.
When I went out of me, I saw my real being.

Ben bir müddet taklid ile kendimi bildim,
Kendimi beğendim.
Ben o vakitler kendimde idim ama asıl kendi varlığımı
Sezememiş anlayamamıştım.
Çünkü o zaman, ben kendimi görememiş,
Kendimi tanıyamamıştım, sâdece adımı işitmiştim.
Fakat ne zaman ki kendimden çıktım
(benliğimi terk ettim)
Işte asıl o zaman kendimi gördüm
(kendimi buldum.)

A summit rubai. Sometimes when a person is on the journey, they don't need wine to be drunk or music to enjoy the exuberance. Their exhuberance comes from annihilation.

9.

We don't need wine to get drunk.
Harp and rebab* are not necessary
For the joy of our gathering.
We are out of ourselves and, like drunks,
Have fallen on the floor.
But, there is no cupbearer for us,
No musician, no beauty.
*A three-stringed musical instrument

Sarhoş olmak için şaraba ihtiyacımız yok.
Meclisteki neşemiz ceng ve rebâba bağlı değil.
Sarhoşlar gibi kendimizden geçmişiz.
Bizim ne sâkiye, ne çalgıcıya, ne güzele ihtiyacımız var.

Mevlana is referring to real Love. Our worldly love is temporary, symbolic; the beginning and end of love belong in this world. In *fanâ* [annihilation], there is no beginning or end.

10.

آن چشم که خون گشت و غم اور اجغتست
زو خواب طمع مدار کو کی خفتست
بیدار دکین نیز نهایت دارد
ای بی خبر از عشق که این را کفتست

Don't expect sleep from the eyes
That shed tears of blood.
The one who is afflicted by this sorrow
Knows nothing about Love
If he thinks that there will be an end of it.

Kanlı yaşlarla dalan, kedere eş olan bir gözden
Sen uyku bekleme. Böyle bir göz, nasıl uyuyabilir?
Ondaki bu uykusuzluk halinin geçeceğini sanarak,
Ona uykusu gelince uyur diyen kişiye
"Sen aşktan habersiz olduğun için böyle
Söylüyorsun" de.

This rubai refers to something that happens on the journey of annihilation, of climbing the mountain: An aspirant becomes restless, becomes very uneasy with the world, with existence.

If someone doesn't know this mountain symbol, they won't have any idea about Mevlana. This is why Mevlana is still unknown: To know him, one has to climb the mountain. A blind person who has touched one small part of an elephant still has no idea about the whole.

11.

أن اكه خذاى جون تو بارى داد ست
او رادلى جان بى قرارى داد ست
زنهار طمح مدار زانكس كا رى
زبراكه خذاش طرنه كارى داد

When God gives such a Beloved like you
To someone,
He makes his heart restless and unstable.
Don't expect normal behavior from him.
God assigned him an unusual task with Love.

Allah birisine senin gibi Sevgili verdiğinde,
Onun kalbini, gönlünü huzursuz ve kararsız yapar.
Ondan normal bir davranış bekleme.
Çünkü; Allah, ona aşkla ilgili görülmedik
Bir görev vermiştir.

This mountain-climbing is neither religious nor nonreligious. It is about the one who dies before their body dies. It is the business of reaching non-dualistic perception.

12.

انکس که بر وی خوب او دشک پریست
آمد سحری و بر دلن نگریست
او گریه و من گریه که تا آمد صبح
پرسید کزین هر دو عجب عاشق کیست

That Beauty whose face makes fairies jealous
Came suddenly at early dawn.
He looked at my heart and started crying.
Then, I started crying too.
Morning came and wondered,
"Who of us is the lover, and who is the Beloved?"

Perilerin bile yüzünü kıskandığı güzel,
Güneş doğarken aniden geldi.
Gönlüme baktı ve ağlamaya başladı.
Sonra, ben de ağlamaya başladım.
Sabah geldi ve dedi ki:
"Bunların hangisi seven, hangisi sevilen?"

This is a description of non-dualistic perception, which occurs only with the completion of *fanâ* [annihilation].

Dualistic perception is what most people think of as normal. People think many have lived here before us and many will come after us. But, in fact, we create this earth, this world, and we think we own it.

This is why we are afraid of dying. We think this world will change after we leave it. We think that when we're in our grave, we will still be prey to worms, ants, all kinds of animals. We forget, believing death is for somebody else.

In fact, our addiction to being and becoming is mankind's biggest problem.

13.

اركفروناسلام برون صحرايست
مارابميان آن فضاسودايست
عارف جوبنان رسيد سررا بنهد
نے كفرونه اسلام ندآنجاجا

There is a plain beyond Islam and heresy.
Our Love stands in the middle of that plain.
The sage will prostrate there,
Because there is room
For neither Moslem nor nonbeliever there.

İslamın ve kâfirliğin ötesinde bir ova vardır.
Sevgimiz bu ovanın ortasındadır.
Arif, orada secde eder.
Burada Müslümana ve kâfire yer yoktur.

This rubai is the description of existence and life, our human story created by our dualistic perception.

14.

ازنوح سفينه ايست ميراث نجات
كردآن وروان ميانه بحرحيات
اندردل ازان جربرسَتَن بنّات
اماجون دل نه نقشرد اردنه جهات

We inherited a boat from Noah
As the prize of deliverance.
It sails through storms on the sea of life.
Thoughts, images, sorrows, and pleasures
Are the reeds over this sea,
But they have neither shape nor direction
Like the heart.

Nuh'tan kurtuluş mirası olarak bir gemi kaldı.
Yaşam denizinde, fırtınalarla dolaşır durur.
Gönlümüzdeki düşünceler, hayaller, gamlar
Ve zevkler denizin üzerinde sazlar gibidir.
Gönül gibi ne şekilleri vardır ne de yönleri.

A summit rubai. It tells everything as it is when one reaches non-dualistic perception. This is *fanâ* [annihilation].

15.

امروزمن وجام صبوحی دردست
می فتم وی خیزم ومی کردم ست
با سروبلند خوبش من مستم و پست
من نیست شوم تا بنود جزوی هست

I exist; a glass of morning wine exists
In my hand today.
I am thinking and walking around.
I am drunk, lowered myself
In front of my tall cypress, my Beloved,
Annihilating myself so that no one would exist
Except Him.

Bugün ben varım, bir de elimde sabah şarabının
Kadehi.
Düşüp, kalkıp etrafta yürüyorum.
Sarhoşum ve selvi boylu Sevgilinin önünde
Alçalıyorum.
Kendimi yok ediyorum ki O'ndan başkası
Var olmasın.

Another rubai from Mevlana after he has reached the summit of the mountain, after he has reached Essence. Very truly this describes the summit, *fanâ* [annihilation].

16.

اندردلن درون وبيرون همه اوست
اندرتن من جانك رك وخون بهااوست
اينجای جكونه كفروايمان كنجد
نے جون باشد وجودمز جون اوست

He is inside and outside of my heart.
He is the soul of my body.
He is my blood and my veins.
How could faith or heresy fit here?
I am absent; He is all of my existence.

O, benim gönlümün içonde ve dışında.
O, benim bedenimin ruhu.
O, benim kanım, o benim damarlarım.
Buraya iman veya kâfirlik nasıl sığar?
Ben yokum. O, benim bütün varığım.

What's the difference between science and Love, existence and non-existence, a scientist and a sage? Research is like a dog chasing its tail, because it's the brain trying to understand the brain. Non-dualistic perception can only be reached through annihilation of the self. We say, "A scientist says what he thinks, while a sage describes what he sees."

17.

اى بنده بدانك خواجه سرق اينست
ازا برکه باد ازل برق اينست
تو هرجه بکوبى انقياسى کوبى
او قصه زديه مى کند فرق اينست

O mortal, this is the Master of all the East.
This is the lightning from the cloud
That scatters pearls.
Whatever you say is based just on reasoning.
Yet, He tells what he sees, and that's the difference.

A kul, bil ki doğunun bilgesi budur.
İnciler yağdıran buluttan çakan şimşek gibidir.
Sen ne söylüyorsan aklınla söylüyorsun.
O, gördüğünü anlatıyor. İşte aradaki fark budur.

Mevlana describes Absence and existence so beauti-fully in so many rubais. How can you miss it?

18.

اى جان جهان جان وجهان باقى نيست
جز عشق قديم شاهد وساقى نيست
بر كعبهٔ نيستى طوا فى دار ذ
عاشق جو ز كعبه است أ فاقى نيست

O soul, O universe, souls and the universe
Are temporary.
There is no beauty, no cupbearer except Eternal Love.
The Lover turns around the Kaaba* of Absence.
He is from that Kaaba, not from the surroundings.

* Cubical temple of Mecca; direction of prayer

A can, a cihan; can da cihan da geçicidir.
Güzellik ve sâkî yoktur. Ancak sonsuz Âşk vardır.
Âşık, yokluk Kâbesini tavaf eder, durur.
O yokluk Kâbe'sindendir, başka yerden değil.

When a person travels up the mountain to annihilate the self, suffering is critical. Fasting, breathing and suffering. To kill the self, you have to suffer. This is it.

19.

ای دل تو ودر د او که درمان اینست

غم میخور ودم مزن که فرمان اینست

گر پای بر آرزو نهادی کجند

کشتی سگ نفس کا که قربان اینست

O heart, here you are, next to His trouble, too.
That's what the cure is: Suffer, don't talk.
That's the commandment.
When you step on the head of your desire,
The dog-self will be suffocated.
That's what the sacrifice is.

A gönül, bir sen varsın, bir de O nun derdi.
Dermanda budur işte.
Gamlar ye, bir söz etme, buyruk böyle.
Dileklerin başına birazcık bastın mı,
Köpek nefsi boğazladın gitti.
Kurban da budur işte.

In dualistic perception, everything, including you, exists in your dream. There is God, a lover, a wound, blood. But, in non-dualistic perception, there is nothing.

20.

This Love is such a Sultan, but his banner is invisible.
This is such a Koran, but its ayats* are invisible.
This hunter wounds every lover,
 But the blood from this wound is invisible.
*The Arabic word for sign or miracle; usually refers to each verse in the
Qur'an [Koran]

Bu Âşk bir sultandır ki,
Bayrağı görünmez.
Bu bir Kuran'dır ki, ayetleri görünmez.
Aşk avcısı her Âşığı yaralar; kanı akar ama
Yarası görünmez.

Another clear description of *fanâ* [annihilation]. In *fanâ*, there is no bad and good, no short and long, no God and creatures.

21.

بر هر جا یی که سر نهم مسجود اوست
در شش جهت و بیرون شش مسجود آن
باغ و گل و بلبل و سماع و شاهد
این جمله بهانه ست هم مقصود اوست

Wherever I put my head down on the ground,
He is the One who is prostrated.
He is the one worshiped in six dimensions and beyond.
All I speak about—
The rose gardens, nightingales, beauties—
All is just a pretext. He is the only purpose.

Başımı koyduğum her yerde secde edilen O'dur.
Altı boyut ve ötesinde ibadet edilen O'dur.
Gül bahçesi, bülbül ve güzel.
Bunların hepsi bahanedir.
Maksat hep O'dur.

Without *fanâ* [annihilation], everything in the world exists: We hate the world; we love the world. Either way, the world becomes our goal. We have a fear of dying: We like our body, our self so much that we don't want to throw it into the ground. *Fanâ* is the medicine for all of this. If a person reaches *fanâ*, they see that everything in the world is just a dream.

22.

بَچَادَه تَرَازِ عَاشِقِ لِ صَبِرِكِجَا سِت
كَبِن عِشِقِ كِرِفَنَارِي بِي هِجِ دَوَاسِت
دِرِمَان عِمِ عِشِق نَه بَخِلاوِ نَه دِرْيَا سِت
دِرِ عِشِقِ حَقِيقَي نَه وِفَاوِ نَه جَفَا سِت

Who is more frustrated than an impatient lover?
There is no cure for Love's sickness.
Goodness and badness don't help the sorrow of Love.
There is neither fidelity nor cruelty in real Love.

Kim, sabırsız bir aşıktan daha çaresiz olabilir?
Aşk hastalığının devası yoktur.
Aşk gamına, ne iyilik ne de kötülük fayda eder.
Gerçek aşkta ne vefâ vardır ne de cefâ.

The "pretty ones" love this world; they are always busy trying to maintain their presence in it. But, this business is about Absence, not existence. To reach Absence there is a price, and it's one that they are not willing to pay.

23.

بیرون زجهان کفروایمان جایست
کاخانه مقام هرتر ورعنا یست
جان بایدداد ودل بشکرانهٔ جان
آنراکه تمنای چنین ما وا پست

There is a place beyond faith and heresy
That is not for all the young and pretty ones
Who want to get there.
One has to give up their life and sacrifice their heart
As the price.

İnancın ve kâfirliğin ötesinde bir yer vardır.
Orası, her tecrübesiz genç ve güzelin yeri değildir.
Oraya ulaşmayı isteyen kişi, hayatını fedâ
Etmeli ve gönlünü bağışlamalıdır.

This earthly rubai stands at the bottom of the mountain. Mevlana notices that the earth looks like it's sleeping, when it's actually getting ready for spring.

24.

نا ظر نبری که این زمین بیهوشست
بیدار و دوچشم بسته چون خرکو
چون دیک هزار کف بسری آرد
نا خلق بدانند که او درجوشست

This earth makes you think
That it has no mind or consciousness.
It acts like it's sleeping; its eyes are closed.
Yet, it is awake and alive, like you are, like I am.
Foam floats on the surface in a boiling saucepan
The same way flowers and plants
Spurt out from the heart of nature.

Şu yeryüzünün, aklı ve bilinci olmadığını
Düşünürsün. Uyuyormuş gibi yapar.
Gözleri kapalıdır, ancak senin ve benim gibi
Ayıktır ve canlıdır.
Köpük, kaynar tencerenin yüzeyine çıkar.
Çiçeklerin ve bitkilerin, doğanın kalbinden
Fışkırdığı gibi.

Annihilation is not a part-time job. An aspirant on the journey must give all on the way to Essence. Existence has to become Essence. Mevlana says over and over again, "The one who is world-hungry doesn't understand me."

25.

نامَن بزيم پيشه وكارم اينست
صَيْد انيم صَيْد وشكارم اينست
روزم اينست روزكارُم اينست
آرام وقرار وغمكسارُم اينست

This is my work, my business and my art
As long as I live.
This is my game, my prayer.
This is my day, my time.
This is my comfort, my confidant.

Yaşadığım sürece sanatım, işim, gücüm budur.
Avcılığım, avlanmam, avım budur.
Günüm, zamanım budur.
Rahatım, huzurum dert ortağım budur.

While you are looking for your Essence, your Essence is looking for you, and one day, your Essence grabs you. "If you take one step towards me, I take a thousand steps towards you." When I say to God, "Where are You?" God answers, "Where are you?"

26.

When Love of the peerless Beloved covered me,
His alchemy turned me from copper into gold.
I was looking for him with not one,
But thousands of hands.
Then, He suddenly grabbed my feet.

Eşsiz Sevgilinin Aşkı beni kaplayınca,
O'nun simyası* beni bakırdan altına çevirdi.
O'nu bir elle değil, binlerce elle arıyordum.
O benim ayağımı aniden tuttu.
*Eski kimya ilimi

Repenting is a revolting against God. It means you are looking for something beyond God, when exactly where you are is God. Repenting is a sin... the biggest sin.

27.

توبه جكنم كه توبه ام رساية تست
يا و سر توبه جمله سرماية تست
برتر كنهى پيش تو توبه بود
كوآن تو به كه لايق پاية تست

Why should I repent?
My repentance comes from You.
The head and feet of repentance are entirely
Your attainments.
It is the biggest sin to repent in front of You.
Does any repentance deserve Your greatness?

Neden tövbe edeyim ki? Tövbelerim Senden geliyor.
Tövbelerin başı da, ayağı da tümüyle Senin marifetin.
Senin önünde tövbe etmek en büyük günahtır.
Hiçbir tövbe Senin büyüklüğüne değer mi?

Your Essence is everything. Your Essence is much bigger than God. Your Essence starts with the world, goes beyond the world, and beyond God. This journey up to the summit of the mountain goes from you to God, through God, beyond God.

28.

آهن سنگ ادن آن بادیة گرد

The world isn't worth half a grain of barley.
You are the gold mine.
You are the Essence and the purpose of the universe.
Everything is created for You.
If the world were illuminated by torches and candles,
What would be their use without a lighter?
The wind would put them out.

Dünya, yarım arpa tanesi bile etmez.
Sen altın madenisin.
Sen, bu dünyanın aslı ve amacısın.
Her şey senin için yaratıldı.
Dünyayı, meşaleler ve mumlar aydınlatsaydı, çakmak
Olmadan bunlar ne işe yarardı.
Rüzgar esince de hepsi sönerdi.

Mevlana brings up fasting again and again. It is one of the tools that carry you on the journey up the mountain.

29.

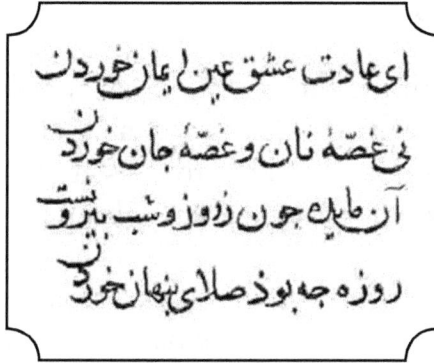

It is customary for Love to eat faith like a meal.
Love goes after neither bread nor the worries of life.
Its table is set beyond day or night.
Then what is fasting?
It is an invitation to a secret feast.

Aşkın huyu, iman kaynağından yemek yemektir.
Aşk ne ekmek derdine düşer, ne can kaygısına.
O yemek, geceden de dışarıdadır, gündüzden de.
Öyleyse oruç nedir? Gizli yemeğe çağrıdır.

We have nothing but our Essence, and it is everything. Humans think of themselves as very important. But, as one has said, "Humans are the statues of perception. They represent infinite layers of limited awareness of the totality."

This could be applied to humans, rocks, plants, animals, everything. Like them, we have a very short stop in this world, really, just a blink of an eye. We all come from nothing and return to nothing.

Many books have been written about the immortal soul, about man and the glory of the world, but nothing has been written comparing the world of infinity with unknown Truth.

We don't take this world—or God—seriously. Our Essence is much bigger than that. It comes from infinity and goes to infinity.

30.

چیزیست که درتوبے توجویازویست
درحال نودریست که ازکان ویست
مائندہ کوی اسپچوکان و ست
آن داردوان داردوآن آن ویست

You have something that is looking for
Him without you.
A pearl which came from His mine
Is lying on your ground.
He is the One who is riding your horse,
And your ball in front of His club belongs to Him!
Belongs to Him!

Sende bir şey var ki, sensiz O nu aramakta.
O'nun madeninden çıkan bir inci var ki senin
toprağındandır.
O senin atına binmiş ve senin topun
O'nun çevgeninin önündedir.
O O'nundur, o O'nundur, o ancak O'nundur.

61

Our Heart is a human's special place. Everything is contained in the human heart. We know every unlimited thing in a limited way; all of it goes into a man's heart. This is why *fanâ* [annihilation] is so important: Without *fanâ*, people treasure unworthy things like wealth, health, fame, and beauty—all things we have to give up if we are to reach something truly worthy.

31.

خورشید رخت زآسمان بیرونست
چون حسن تو کز شرح زبان بیرون
خیز بد کآن لطیف قامت برخاست
خیز بد که امروز قیامت برخاست

Beloved, the sun of Your face
Doesn't fit in the skies;
Your Beauty can't be described by words.
Your Love is beyond the universe,
Yet, it made my heart its home.

Sevgili, yüzünün güneşi gökyüzüne sığmaz.
Senin güzelliğin kelimelerle anlatılamaz.
Senin aşkın kâinata sığmazken,
Gönlüme sığdı, orasını evi yaptı.

It's difficult to add anything to what this rubai says. But, simply to reiterate, you can't get real knowledge from any school or book or experiment or study. Unless you annihilate your self, all knowledge you gain is false. It's not about learning; it's about unlearning.

32.

در مجلس عشاق قراری دگرست

وین بادهٔ عشق را خماری دگرست

آن علم که در مدرسه حاصل گردد

کاری دگرست و عشق کاری دگرست

There is a different air in the gathering of Lovers,
A different drunkenness from Love's wine.
Knowledge you learned from the medrasa* is one thing,
But Love is different.
*Muslim theological school

Aşıkların meclisinde başka bir hava vardır.
Aşkın şarabında başka bir sarhoşluk vardır.
Medresede öğrendiğin bilgi ile
Aşkta öğrendiklerin başkadır.

People want to be handsome or beautiful, healthy, wealthy, happy. They don't care about walking on this path paved with fire. But, "healthy, wealthy, happy" is for the animal in us. In order to reach Essence, "healthy, wealthy, happy" is only the beginning.

33.

درنه قدم ارجه راه نی پایا نست
کز دور نظاره کار نامردانست
این راه زز ندگی دل حاصل کن
کین زندگی تن صفت حوانست

Step on the road that has no end to it.
Watching from the distance is not for a man.
Start the journey with the strength of the heart.
The body's strength is for animals.

Sonu olmayan yola adım at.
Uzaktan izlemek, insana yakışmaz.
Gönlün gücüyle yolculuğa çık.
Beden gücü hayvanlar içindir.

Suffering is what makes the fire which burns out the unnecessary parts of you. It burns all the trash and brings out the gold. It annihilates your self and carries you to Essence.

34.

دلخسته وزارونا توانم زغمت
خونا به زدیك می برانم زغمت
هرجند یلب رسیدجانم زغمت
غمگین کردم جوباز مانم زغمت

I wail and cry because of Your sorrow.
Your sorrow forces bloody tears from my eyes.
I am about to die because of Your sorrow.
But, I am sorrowful so that some day
I might be out of Your sorrow.

Kederinden gönlüm yaralı, ağlayıp duruyorum.
Güçsüzüm, perişanım, dermansızım.
Derdinden canım dudaklarıma geldi,
Fakat derdinden ayrılacağım diye dertlenip duruyorum.

In modern times, everyone talks about the importance of "know your self." Unfortunately, to get to know your self takes you down a dead-end street. Your self keeps you in one trouble after another. To "know your Essence" is a much better term. And, you have to annihilate your self to reach your Essence.

35.

سرمايهٔ عقل سرّ ديوانگيست
ديوانهٔ عشق مرد فرزانگيست
آنكس كه شذ آشناى دل درد درد
با خويشتنش هزار بيگانگيست

An asset of wisdom is a secret of Love's madness.
Love's insane one is the wisest man in the world.
If one learns the heart's mysteries
By the way of suffering,
He becomes a stranger a thousand times to himself.

Bilgeliğin özü, Aşk deliliğin sırrıdır.
Aşkın delisi, en bilge kişidir.
Gönlün sırlarını, acı çekerek öğrenen,
Kendisine binlerce kez yabancı olur.

So many people think Mevlana never mentions Absence. Yet, here is his most basic statement: This business is about Absence, not existence.

36.

سر لیست ده عشق ودر ودعوی نیست
زیراکه صفا ت وعجز معنی نیست
مر عاشق راجواب از فتوی نیست
این مسٔله نیستیست از هستی نیست

There is neither question nor answer
On the way to Love,
But only a mystery.
The lover never answers to the Fatwa.*
This is a matter of Absence, not existence.
Term in Islamic faith for a legal opinion or learned interpretation

Aşk yolunda ne soru, ne de cevap vardır.
Sadece sır vardır.
Aşık, fetva dinlemez.
Bu konu yokluk meselesidir, varlık meselesi değil.

At the end of the world of existence is the world of Absence, which can only be reached by total annihilation of the self. Most readers of Mevlana and Mevlana scholars talk about Love in Rumi, but they think of it, present it in human terms. The Love Mevlana talks about is in the world of Absence, and it is far from human love. He can talk about this Love because he has reached the summit of the mountain: He is a man of Absence, not of existence.

37.

عشق توفي در اطراف كيانى بى تاخت
مسكين دلن دبد نشانئ بشناخت
روزى كه دلم زبند هستى برهد
در كنم عدم چه عشقها خواهم باخت

While Your Love was riding a horse on the plains,
My heart recognized You through secret signs.
When I free myself from the bonds of existence,
What wonderful Love games my heart
Will play with You
In the land of Absence.

Aşkın, ovada at sürerken, zavallı gönlüm
Gizli işaretlerle O'nu tanıdı.
Gönlüm varlık bağından kurtulduğu gün,
Yokluk âleminde Seninle ne aşk oyunları oynayacak.

Reason (the mind) challenges lovers. A lover is the one who is in *fanâ* [annihilation], who is annihilating his self. This rubai presents the dichotomy of reason and Love (ecstasy).

38.

عقل آمد پند عاشقان بیش کرفت
در ره بنشست و ره زنی بیش کرفت
چون در سرشان جایگه بند ندید
پای مه بوسید و سر خویش کرفت

Reason came to advise the lovers.
It sat in the middle of the road
And stopped them one by one.
But, when it realized it couldn't find a place
In the minds of the lovers,
It kissed their feet and left.

Akıl, aşıklara öğüt vermeye geldi.
Yolun ortasında oturdu ve aşıkları taker teker durdurdu.
Ancak, aşıkların kafalarında öğüt alacak
Bir yer bulamayınca, âşıkların ayaklarını öptü
Ve başını alıp gitti.

People talk about themselves and others, but they don't know themselves, and they don't know others. They talk a lot about God. They say, "God, I love you." They say, "God forbids me to do such and such." God this way, God that way. But, they don't know anything about God.

39.

قومی غمكین وخود مدان عم زكماس
قومی شادان ولی حبر كان جه حا
جلدین جپ وراست خبر ازجب وَیا
جلدین من وما ست خبر ازنر وِیا

Sad or merry, people don't know
The source of sorrow and joy.
Some go left, some go right,
But they have no idea of left and right.
They say, "I am,"and "We are,"
But they don't know who they are.

Gamlı veya neşeli, insanlar gamın ve
Neşenin nereden geldiğini bilmezler.
Bazıları bu tarafa gider, bazıları ise o tarafa
Ancak nereye gittiklerinden haberleri yoktur.
"Ben" veya "Biz" derler, ancak kim
Olduklarını bilmezler.

Humans are familiar with the word, "particle" because of quantum physics. This rubai is actually far better than the Big Bang theory, far better than anything. Creation of the universes comes from Love, from Absence.

40.

If grief covers everything,
The one who grabs Love becomes carefree.
Look at the particle: When he touched Love,
He turned into such a shape that created universes.

Bütün dünyayı gam, keder kaplasa,
Aşka tutunan kişi, gamsızdır.
Zerreye bak: Aşka dokunduğu zaman,
Öyle bir hale geldi ki iki dünyayı da yarattı.

When one reaches *fanâ* [annihilation], they put together good and bad, pretty and ugly, right and wrong. All the opposites merge. This is the iron face Mevlana is referring to: One reflects, one doesn't see. Unless there is a mirror, you don't see yourself. I am a mirror to you. This is it.

41.

كرشرم هي ازان واين بايدداشت
بس عيب كسان زير زمين بايدداشت
ورآ ينه وار نيك وبد بنما هي
جون آينه روى آهين بايدداشت

If someone is ashamed of this and that,
That someone has to bury people's faults underground.
In order to reflect good and evil like a mirror,
You must have an iron face like a mirror.

Eğer şundan bundan utanılıyorsa,
İnsanların kusurlarını yer altına gömmek gerek.
Eğer bir ayna gibi iyiyi, kötüyü göstereceksen,
Sana ayna gibi demirden bir yüz gerek.

From the beginning of life, everybody has desires, and they go in every direction to satisfy those desires, to get all the pleasures out of their life. But, the real source of desire, of pleasure is unknown.

42.

كس نيست كه اندرهوسى نيست
كس نيست كه اندرسرش اين سودا
سررشته آن ذوق كزوحنيزدشوق
پيداست كه هستان ولى پيدا نيست

Everyone is crazy with some desire;
There is a love in everyone's head.
The pleasure that creates the yearning is obvious,
But the source of the pleasure is obscure.

Herkes bir hevesle deli divane olmuş.
Başında bir sevda bulunmayan yok.
Özlemi yaratan zevk, apaçık ortada.
Ancak, zevkin kaynağı gizli.

Left and right represent the stage of dualistic perception. In non-dualistic perception, there is no left or right.

43.

كفتند كه سن حهت همه نورحدا ست
فربا دزخلق خا ست كان نورگأ ست
بيكانه نظركرد لهرسوجب ودا ست
كفتنددى نظريكن حب ودا ست

They said: "God's brilliance
Shines from six dimensions."
People cried and asked: "Where is the light?"
Then, the people looked to the left and to the right.
"One second," they said again,
"Look at it, but without left or right."

Dediler ki: "Altı yönden de Allah'ın nuru parlamakta."
İnsanlar ağlayıp, sordular: Nur nerede?"
Sağ ve sollarına bakıp, nuru göremediler.
Bir ses onlara dedi ki: "Bir anda sağsız ve solsuz bakın."

Soul's sugar is very unique. Nobody would ever expect an animal to appreciate it.

44.

We are the lovers of Love; Love is our salvation.
Soul resembles Hizir;* Love, the Water of Life.
Alas to one who is not decorated by the Sultan of Love.
How does an animal know soul's sugar?
*Legendary Godsend who attained immortality by drinking from the Water
of Life; comes to aid in a critical moment

Biz âşkın âşıklarıyız. Âşktır bizim kurtuluşumuz.
Can, Hızır'a benzer, Aşk da Ab-i hayata.
Yazıklar olsun âşkın Sultanından berate olmayana.
Hayvan ne anlar, can şekerinden?

A person who reaches their Essence is not world-hungry; they are obliged to God. The one who is blessed with the glory of finding Essence is born like that, is made like that, is obliged to God from birth.

Some people are obliged to money, to fame, to beauty, to God time-by-time. They are born like that, and they are happy traveling in their world.

One who is completely obliged to God doesn't read books, listen to lectures, or go to school to find their Essence. They climb the mountain.

Reaching *baka* [nothingness] is the end of *fanâ* [annihilation]. It is *ke-en lem yekün* ["as if it were not"]. You have to be completely obliged to God to get there.

45.

مروصل نراهزارصاحب هوسراست
ناخود بوصال نوكرا نست دست
انكركه يا فت راحتى يافت تما م
وآن كس كه نيافت رنج نا يافتست

Thousands are eager to find You,
But unless You give them Your hand,
No one can reach You.
The one who finds You will gain Your compassion.
The one who does not will be happy
With the trouble of searching for You.

Binlercesi, Seni bulmak için sabırsızlanır.
Ancak, onlardan elini verdiğin Sana ulaşır.
Seni bulan kişi, Senin şefkatine erişir.
Seni bulamayan ise Seni arama zahmetine
Girdiği için mutludur.

This rubai may sound like existential monism, but it is actually more than that. So many people talk about the union of existence, but existence is a very low-grade concept. This rubai is a semi-earthly rubai. Often when Mevlana finds himself saying things that may sound strange to people, he likes to excuse himself, letting them know that it is God saying them.

46.

من كوهم و قال من صداى يارست
من نقشم و نقش بندم آن دلدارست
چون قفل كه در بانك درايذ زكليد
مى پندارى كه كفت من كفتارست

I am a mountain; I am echoing the Beloved.
I am a painting; that Beloved is my painter.
Do you think all these words I've said belong to me?
No, they are the sound of the key turning in the lock.

Ben bir dağım, sesim Sevgilinin yankısı.
Ben bir resimim.
Sevgili benim ressamım.
Bütün söylediğim sözler bana ait değildir.
Bunlar kilidi döndüren anahtarın sesi.

Annihilation of self is poverty in every way. Poverty owns everything.

47.

نكرفت دلت زانك تراد دل نكرفت
انرا كه كرفت دل عم كل نكرفت
باري كلمن جز صفت دل نكرفت
بى حاصليم جز ده حاصل نكرفت

Since you didn't take care of the heart,
It didn't hold your hands,
And you didn't get a fair share of Love.
You can't love just anyone!
When the heart holds a person's hands,
That person won't fall in the mud of lowly desires.
Not even once did my rose get its smell or color
From anyone but heart. I have nothing in my hand,
But this poverty made me own everything.

Sen gönül sahibi olmadığından, gönül senin
Elinden tutmadı ve âşktan bir pay alamadın.
Sevmek mutluluğuna eremedin. Gönül, birisinin
Elini tuttuğunda, o kişi tutkuların çamuruna düşmez.
Benim gülüm, kokusunu ve rengini gönülden
Başka kimseden almadı.
Elimde hiçbir şey yok. Ancak, yokluk her şeye ve
Âşk'a sahip olmama neden oldu.

95

Quantum physics accepts this concept.

48.

هر ذره که در هوا و در کبوا نست
بر ما همه گلشن و سبستا نست
هر جند که زر زر را همای کا نست
هر قطره طلسمیت در و عا نست

Every particle in the air is an apple orchard
And a rose garden to us.
Though gold comes from gold mines,
There is a golden spell in every drop
That conceals an ocean.

Havada ki her zerre, bize elma ve gül bahçesidir.
Altın, altın madeninden gelir ama, her
Damlada, bir okyanusu gizleyen altın
Büyüsü vardır.

A semi-earthly rubai in which Mevlana explains that his capacity cannot cover everything.

49.

هر روز دل مرا سماع وطر بیست
می گوید حسنش که برین بزمه ایست
کویندجراخوری نوبانج انکشت
زیرا انکشت پنج آمد شش نیست

have a joyous, pleasurable sema every day in my heart.
But, His beauty tells me, "Don't stop there. Go further."
Some people ask me, "Why do you eat with five fingers?
Because I only have five fingers, not six.

Gönlümde her gün, zevkli ve neşeli bir semâ var.
Ancak, O'nun güzelliği der ki:
"Burada durma. Bunu da yeterli bulma."
"Neden beş parmakla yiyorsun?" diyorlar.
Beş parmağım var, altı parmağım yokta ondan.

Our worship of God through actions like prayer, good works, sacrifices, rituals and anything else actually represents our efforts to bribe God. We want God to take care of us in this world and in heaven. But, God doesn't have anything to do with that. For God, a lame donkey and a strong horse are the same. Mevlana says that anyone who annihilates their self and reaches *fanâ* will see that. This rubai will probably disappoint a lot of people.

50.

ماری کہ مِن دا وکلِ وظار یکسِت
در مذهب او مصحف و زنار یکسِت
مارا عِم آں، یار جرا با یہ دحو ر د
کزراخ لتکہ داسب دهوار یکسِت

He is such a Beloved that a rose and a thorn
Are the same for Him.
In His religion, the Koran and the Bible are the same.
Don't try to impress Him.
A lame donkey and a fleet of horses
Are the same for Him.

O öyle bir Sevgili ki, O'nun nazarında gül ve diken aynıdır.
O'nun dininde Kuran ve zünnar* aynıdır.
O'nu yorumlamaya çalışma.
Çünkü O'nun nazarında topal eşekle yörük at aynıdır.
*13.yüzyılda Hiristiyan kesişlerin bellerine bağladıkları kuşak

This very earthly rubai represents the bottom of the mountain. The lover and Beloved are separated and personalized. One of the lover's eyes is very much involved with the Beloved, while the other is not. At the Summit, lover and Beloved are the same.

51.

يك چشم من از روز جدايى بگريست
چشم دگرم گفت چرا گريه زچيست
چون روز وصال شد مرا نش كردم
گفتم نگرسينى بنايد نگريست

On the day of separation, one of my eyes was crying.
"Why are you crying?" the other eye asked.
At union, the wet eye said to the dry one:
"Don't look at the Beloved. You don't deserve it."

Ayrılık gününde, gözlerimden bir tanesi ağlıyordu.
"Neden ağlıyorsun?" diye diğer gözüm sordu.
Buluşma gününde yaşlı göz, diğer kuru olana dedi ki:
"Sevgiliye bakma. O'nu, sen hak etmedin."

Another bottom-of-the mountain rubai. Mevlana is trying to be excused because of his wine drinking. As he says, however, the wine he drinks is not from grapes.

52.

O one who denies my wine-drinking,
Don't think that this wine is coming from grapes.
My enthusiasm is my wine; my heart is my glass.
My cupbearer is the One
Who illuminates the darkness every morning.

Ey, beni aşk şarabımı içmemi kınayan
Kişi, şarabım bağcının ektiği üzümden değil.
Coşkunluğum şarabımdır; gönlüm kadehimdir.
Her sabah, karanlığı aydınlatansa sâkîmdir.

This rubai has a similar message to another rubai in which God advises his prophet not to sit next to anyone except lovers.

53.

آنجا بنشین که منشین مردانند
تا دود کدورتِ ترا بنشانند
اندیشه مکن بعیبِ ایشان کایشان
زان پیشترکه اندیشه کنی دانند

Sit next to God's lovers.
They will clear your confusion
And clean the smoke of your sorrow.
Don't ever think badly about them,
Because they will know your thoughts
Before you think them.

Allah aşıklarının yanına otur.
Bulanıklığını arıtsınlar, gam dumanını temizlesinler.
Onlar hakkında hiçbir zaman kötü düşünme.
Çünkü onlar, düşüncelerini, senden önce bilirler.

A rubai from the bottom of the mountain in which Mevlana presents some earthly findings.

54.

آنرا که بعلم وعقل اۤ فراشته اند
آن را بحساب روذی انگاشته اند
آن را که سر از عقل نهی داشته اند
از مال بجای آن درانباشته اند

When fate gives knowledge and intelligence
To someone,
It cuts his sustenance and makes him poor.
It fills the ignorant one with wealth instead of wisdom,
And turns him into a storehouse or a granary.

Kader birine bilgi ve akıl verdiğinde,
Onun kısmetini keser, darlık verir.
Cahile bilgelik yerine mal vererek onu
Ambara çevirir.

When someone is presented with wisdom they don't understand, they don't listen. Rather than subjecting them to boredom, they simply aren't invited back. An earthly rubai.

55.

آن روز که مهرکان کرده و زنده اند
مهر زر عاشقان دکر کوزنده اند
کافدل خون خواره دره زر بیاند
وز مکر جنین زاهد و عابد شناند

When they arranged and appraised the world,
They put a different seal on the lover's gold.
You'll never understand this business,
Because the most valuable treasure was tossed out
From the palace of mind.

Yeryüzünü değerlendirdikleri gün,
Aşıkların altınlarına farklı bir damga bastılar.
Bu işi hiçbir zaman anlayamazsın.
En değerli hazine olan bu altınları, onlar
Aklın sarayından fırlatıp attılar.

Everybody is looking for a special male or female friend who is made out of mud, out of clay. If they find one, they'll like him or her, love him or her. That's fine. But, if they would find somebody who is not made out of mud, is divine, they would be happier. I believe that Mevlana is referring to Shams in this rubai.

56.

 انكسركه زآب وكل زكايه دارذ
روزى بوصال اوقرارى دارذ
اى نادره انك زآب وكل بيرون شذ
كوجون توغريب شهريارى دارذ

When someone who came from mud suddenly finds
A beloved who also came from mud,
He calms down and becomes happy.
But, the best is the one who comes from mud,
Finds the Divine Beloved and attains His Love.

Balçıktan meydana gelmiş birisi,
Sevgilisinin de balçıktan meydana
Geldiğini öğrenince sevinir.
Ancak, balçıktan meydana gelen Senin
Gibi ilahi bir Sevgiliyi bulur ve aşkı elde ederse,
O kişi en mutlu olandır.

113

This is a very earthly rubai. It counsels people not to look for wealth, fame, power.

57.

انکس که زجرخ نیم ناے دارذ
وزبهرمقام آشیاے دارذ
نی طالب کس بوذ نه مطلوب کسے
کو سادرے که خوس جهای دارذ

The one who has half a loaf of bread
And a small place to stay,
The one who asks no one and is asked by no one,
He is the happiest, because he lives with Your joy
And has the best of the worlds.

Yarım ekmeği ve oturabileceği ufak bir yuvası olan,
Ne kimseyi soran, ne de kimsenin sormadığı kişi,
En mutlu olandır.
Çünkü Senin mutluluğunla yaşar ve onun
Kendine göre hoş bir dünyası vardır.

115

This rubai is from the middle of the mountain, half earthly, half divine. It's impossible to change your destiny. Once you get on this path, you'll stay on it. Sometimes, you'll want to quit and become earthly, but it's impossible. There are secret pursuers that want to keep you on the path. Sooner or later you realize that this path is your destiny and theirs, too.

58.

آنها که شب و روز ترا با شرند
صیّاد نهانند ولی محتصرند
با هرکه بسازی توازانت بَبرند
گر تو نَ روی کشان کشان ات بَبرند

You don't know it, but there is someone
Who is watching you day and night.
There are invisible, secret pursuers.
They don't show you their intention,
And they separate you from the One
So that you feel all alone.
And, if you don't go out of yourself,
They will drag you out.

Bilmiyorsun, ancak gece, gündüz seni izleyenler var.
Onlar, görünmeyen, gizli avcılardır.
Sana, niyetlerini göstermezler.
Seni yalnız bırakmak için dostlarından ayırırlar.
Yalnız gitmezsen, seni sürükleyerek götürürler.

This rubai comes from way, way up the mountain. Mevlana is becoming detached from the world. He is feeling the warmness of Love, *fanâ* [annihilation]. His exuberance is Love, and it makes him forget shame and blame. This is the way it feels.

59.

ازآتش عشق سردها کرم شود
ورتا بش عشق سنگها نرم شود
ای دوست گناه عاشقان سخت مگر
کن بازه عشق مریدے شرم شود

Love's fire warms cold hearts and melts stones.
Forgive lovers for their sins, O friend!
A man becomes shameless
When he drinks Love's wine.

Aşk ateşi, soğuk gönülleri ısıtır, taşları eritir.
Ey dost, Âşıkların günahlarını affet.
Çünkü aşk şarabından içenler utanmaz olurlar.

A reminder that patience is needed on the journey. Truth doesn't come like a bolt of lightning. The journey to Truth is like untangling a ball of tangled silk thread: It takes a long, long time. It is not a business of imprudence or impatience.

60.

ازجانب عشق اگر رسولان نبود
ازروني زيركان وكولان نبود
عشق تو جابريشم درهم شذاست
نقّاد ئ آن کار ملولان نبود

If messengers didn't bring help from Love,
How could the smart one and the fool
Sustain themselves?
Your Love is like a tangled silk ball,
Not for the impatient to untie.

Aşkın katından elçiler gelmeseydi, akıllılar ve aptallar,
Rızık alabilirler miydi?
Senin aşkın birbirine dolanmış ipek ipliğe benzer;
Onu açmak, sabırsızların harcı değildir.

Another rubai about the importance of prudence and patience.

61.

ازنے شکرای جان بخدا را سازند
وزبوک درخت توت دیبا سازند
آهسه مکن شتاب صبری بنمای
کز غوره بروزگار حلوا سازند

O my soul, they found the way
To make sugar out of sugarcane.
They weave silk from the matter of mulberry leaves.
Be patient; bitter grapes
Become halva* with time.
*Sweetmeats

Ey canım, şekerkamışından şeker
Yapmanın bir yolunu buldular.
Dut yaprağından ipek kumaş dokudular.
Sabırlı ol, koruk; zamanla helva olur.

Fanâ [annihilation] doesn't happen all at once, at one time. At the beginning, the one who annihilates their self feels *fanâ* come and go. Eventually it becomes permanent. In this rubai, Mevlana is sharing a good day when he is experiencing *fanâ* before it has become permanent.

62.

امروز خوش است انک دلخوش دارد
از جام ازل جان قدح کش دارد
در آب حیات غوطه دارد دل او
تا غم خورد انک در دل آتش دارد

Today is a fine day, a happy and cheerful one.
He who has soul drinks wine from the glass of eternity.
His heart swims in the Water of Life.
The one who carries the fire of Love in his heart
Doesn't care what happens around him.

Bugün, güzel bir gündür; mutlu ve neşeli.
O'nun ezel kadehinden şarap içen bir canı vardır.
Gönlü, bengisuyun içinde dalgalanır.
Gönlünde aşk ateşi olan, hiç gam yer mi?

Another rubai from way, way up the mountain. The Love in this poem is far different from human, symbolic love. A human has intelligence, or mind, but when their transformation is complete, this mind is replaced by Love.

63.

اسُبُ سا قی يمنک می کردان کرد
دل بغا بُردو دست ذرا يان کرد
حندان می لعل ريخت تا طوفان کرد
بکباره وُنا و عقل لا ويرآن کرد

The cupbearer is serving wine not by glasses,
But by pitchers tonight.
He has plundered every heart
And is now looking at faiths.
He has served so much wine
That a flood has taken away the house of mind.

Bu gece sâki şarabı kadehle değil testi ile sunuyor.
Her gönlü yağmaladı, şimdi de imana el atıyor.
O kadar şarap sundu ki, şarap sel oldu,
Aklın evini alıp götürdü.

Science and discussion don't get you anywhere near Truth. You have to go through annihilation—through the door of Absence—to get to Truth. You have to flutter where His birds are. Everything else is gossip.

64.

اى دل ازين بقيل وقالت ندهند
جز بر درنيستى وصالت ندهند
وانكاه دران هوا كه مرغانى اند
تا با پروبالى بروبالت ندهند

O heart, you go nowhere on this road
By talk and gossip.
You can't reach the Beloved
Unless you pass through the door of Absence.
If you don't flutter your wings where His birds fly,
They don't give out wings, O heart.

Ey gönül, bu Aşk yolunda dedikoduyla -
Lafla hiçbir yere varamazsın.
Yokluk kapısından geçmeden, Sevgiliye ulaşamazsın.
O'nun kuşlarının uçtuğu havada kanat çırpmadıkça,
Sana kol, kanat vermezler.

129

Humans have the qualities of water and mud, but they are actually more than that. If a human stays with their human perception, they will stay in the cycle of time, of day and night. The ones who realize this will start the journey of annihilation of self and eventually wake up from the cycle. Otherwise, they'll be sleeping day and night.

65.

اى قوم كه برتر زمه و مهتا نبيد
از هستى آب وكل جرامى نا بيد
اى اهل خراباﺕ كه در عزقا بيد
حيزيد كه روز و شب جرا در خوابيد

O humans, who are better than moon and moonlight,
You've been created from water and mud,
But you are better than they are!
Why are you stuck in the mud?
O drunks of this tavern,
Why are you submerged in water?
Why do you sleep day and night? Wake up!

Ey Ay'dan ve Ay ışığından üstün olan insanlar sudan,
Topraktan yaratılmış olduğu halde,
Sudan da topraktan da üstün olan varlıklar.
Niye bir balçığa saplanıp, kalmışsınız.
A sulara batmış meyhane ehli artık kalkın, artık gece,
Gündüz neden uykudasınız.

Quantum physicists have shown the world the movement, the rotation of atoms, protons, nuclei. Everyone, everything, every particle is turning in this divine rotation.

66.

اين سركه درهن سينه ماى كردد
ازكردش اوجرخ دونامى كردد
بى سردانى زباى بى باى ز سر
اند سروباى سروبا مى كردد

There is a secret in our hearts that keeps turning.
It is the reason for the movement of every creature;
Even the whirling sky depends on it.
That secret doesn't distinguish head from feet;
It keeps turning without heads and feet.

Gönlümüzde dönüp duran bir sır var.
Her varlık ve kat kat gökyüzü O'nun
Dönüşü yüzünden dönüyor.
O sır, ne ayaktan başı, ne de baştan ayağı ayırt ediyor.
Başta ayakta, O sırla başsız ayaksız dönüp duruyor.

A rubai that talks about both the human and the divine. It is an earthly rubai from the bottom of the mountain.

67.

بس دربا لها كان ملح درد شود
بس دولتها كه روي ازان زرد شود
خوش حرا آن بود كزان كرم شوي
خوش آن بود كه كرم ازو سرد شود

There are remedies that are worse than troubles.
There are riches
That can make you poor and destitute.
The fire of God warms you and fills you with joy,
But the fire of that beauty turns you ice cold.

Nice dermanlar vardır, derdinden beter.
Nice devletler vardır, beti benzi soldurur.
Allah korkusu odur ki onunla ısınasın, keyiflenesin.
Yoksa ne güzeller vardır, ateşi soğutur, buz yapar seni.

Everything starts with smell. Everyone is obliged to something: Those obliged to money and beauty smell money and beauty right from the beginning. If somebody isn't born obliged to God, they'll be very earthly. And, everything earthly dies and is forgotten.

In any and every case, this smell is a passive attraction. If somebody is born obliged to God, they need to start the journey and be actively involved in it. The world-hungry will not follow this path.

68.

بوبت آمدكرين دارو وى نماند
برهيز وكرين خن بذان سوى نماند
از بوى تو رنگ و بوى مامى دُزدين
تا كا رجان شد كه زمابوى نماند

Once I got Your smell, I was forced to go Your way.
My color and scent were stolen by Your smell.
I was annihilated at the end,
And nothing was left of me, not even a smell.

Senin kokunu aldım da, Senin yoluna düştüm.
Senin kokun benim rengimi ve kokumu çaldı.
Sonunda yok oldum, bir kokum bile kalmadı.

This rubai focuses on the role of suffering on the path of annihilation [*fanâ*].

69.

بوی دم مقبلان جوگل خوش باشد
بدبخت جوخار تیز وسرکش باشد
درصحبت کل خار زانش بوهد
وز صحبت خار کل در آتش باشد

Exuberant people smell like roses;
Timid ones resemble thorns.
The thorns are not thrown into the fire
Just because they are with a rose.
But, the rose remains in the fire
Because of its proximity to the thorns.

İyi insanların kokuları, gül gibi hoştur.
Bahtı kötü kişilerin ise diken gibi keskindir.
Diken, gülle beraber olduğu için ateşe atılmaz.
Ancak, gül dikenle olduğu için ateşler içindedir.

Without this kind of Love, there would be nothing on earth. Human, symbolic love makes us more earthly, more attached to the earth. You say you love a lot of earthly things, including God. The personification of God is very earthly. How can you love something you don't know? So many people think that the Love Mevlana talks about in so many of his poems is Sham's* love or God's Love or someone else's love. It's not. It's very different than all of that.

Shams of Tebriz met Rumi in Konya, Turkey when Rumi was well over 60 years of age. From the time they met, Rumi's life became the story of Annihilation, from being to Non-being, existence to Non-existence. They spent three years together before Shams disappeared.

70.

عشق نشاط و طرب افزون شود نے
نے عشق وجود خوب و موزون شود
صد قطره زابر آگر بدریا بارد
نے جنبش عشق دُر مکنون شود

There would be no joy or happiness without Love,
No beauty, no harmony in existence.
If even hundreds of raindrops
Fell from the clouds to the sea,
None would conceive a pearl without Love.

Âşksız ne neşe, ne de zevk olur.
Âşksız varlık güzelleşemez, ölçülü bir hale gelemez.
Bulutlardan denize yüzlerce damla yağsa,
Âşk olmadı mı inci meydana gelemez.

Mevlana has so many rubais from the summit of the mountain in which he excuses himself, warning readers that these are not his words, but rather words coming through him. He has completed his transformation, but he is still on earth, living, talking, walking as a human; he has to have this protection.

71.

بے من زدهان من سخن می ایـد
من بے حبرم که انکے فرمـا یـد
زهرو شکرا رذوی مَن بے ایـد
زایـد جه دانـد کـه کرا می ثـا بـد

The words from my mouth don't belong to me.
Although I talk with His words,
I am not aware of them.
Do you think this poison or sugar
Is under my control?
Although they come from my heart,
I don't know to whom they belong.

Ağzımdan çıkan kelimeler bana ait değil.
O ne buyuruyorsa, ben onu söylüyorum.
Benim o kelimelerden haberim bile yok.
Zehir ve şekerin isteğimle geldiğini mi düşünüyorsun?
Onlar gönlümden geliyor, ancak kime ait
Olduğunu ben nasıl bilebilirim ki?

bsence and the self are described so beautifully:
If you stay with your self, you're not going to go any-
where; you'll become nothing more than a morsel for
the ground. Self is a hair in the eye, a thorn in the foot, a
stain in the soul. Only if you go through your self, only
then will you get to "You without you." Anyone who
wants to know Mevlana should read and re-read this
rubai.

72.

They will not allow you to go inside of yourself
While you keep staying with yourself.
Only if you annihilate the self
Will they keep you in their eyes and hearts.
Only if you give up both worlds
Will they stamp you with the seal of Absence.

Sen, sendeyken senden sana yol vermezler.
Kendini yok ettiğin zaman, seni gözlerinde
Ve gönüllerinde tutarlar.
İki dünyadan arınırsan, o zaman seni,
Yokluktadır diye hiçlik mührüyle damgalarlar.

Here Mevlana gives a good description of his biography. He was nobody until Love flared up in his heart. At that point, everything was burned to ashes through self-annihilation. He became poems and gazels and rubais. He became Mevlana.

73.

تا در دل من عشق تو افروخته شد
جز عشق تو هرجه داشتم سوخته شد
عقل و سبق و کتاب بر طاق نهاد
شعر و غزل و د وبیتی آموخته شد

O Beloved, when Your Love flared up in my heart,
Everything else was burned to ashes.
My heart put mind, books, and lessons on the shelf,
Learned poems, gazels, and rubais.

Ey Sevgili, senin Âşkın kalbimde yeşerdiğinde,
Geri kalan her şey yanıp kül oldu.
Kalbim, aklımı, kitaplarımı ve derslerimi rafa kaldırdı.
Şiirler, gazeller ve rubailer öğrendi.

147

A very earthly rubai from the bottom of the mountain. The soul is incarnated in the body, which is made from the four elements of the earth: air, water, earth and fire. Being so close to these four elements makes the soul soiled and dirty. We need to get out so we no longer have such bad neighbors.

74.

After a soul comes into a body,
It becomes a neighbor of four elements:
Air, water, earth and fire.
Just like a good grape gets color from a bad one,
A soul imitates the four elements.
May God give no one bad neighbors!

Ruh, bedene girdiğinde, tabiatın dört
Unsuru ile komşu olur: hava, su, toprak ve ateş.
Nasıl iyi üzüm kötü üzümden renk alırsa,
Ruhta bu dört unsuru taklit eder.
Allah kimseye kötü komşular vermesin.

Very earthly.

75.

تنها مرو که ره زنان بسیارند
یک جان داری و خصم جان بسیارند
خصم جان را جان و جهانی خوانی
جون تو گولان در این جهان بسیارند

Don't travel alone on this road;
There are lots of brigands.
You are only one and the enemies are many,
And you call them friends.
In this world there are as many fools as you.

Hak yolunda yalnız yolculuk etme, yol kesenler çoktur.
Sen teksin, can düşmanlarınsa çok.
Sen düşmanına canım dostum dersin,
Bu dünyada senin gibi aptallar çoktur.

This rubai provides an excellent description of annihilation of self.

76.

نوسج نه و هيج نوبه زوجو د

نوغرو زيا بي وزيا ست هه سود

كو بي كه مراست جز خاك بدست

اى برخاكت حمله افلاك حسود

You are nothing.
But, this nothingness is better than existence.
You are lost in losses, but your loss is better than gain.
"I have nothing but a handful of dust," you said.
But, the skies are envious of that dust.

Sen, bir "hiçsin" ancak hiçlik varlıktan daha iyidir.
Sen, ziyana batmışsın, ancak ziyanın kârdan daha iyidir.
Dedin ki: "Elimde topraktan başka bir şey yok."
Ey benim canım, elindeki toprağa bütün gökyüzü
Hasat ediyor

153

Another excellent description of annihilation of self. Talking doesn't get you anywhere. You have to annihilate your self to reach your Essence, or Truth.

77.

جان باز که وصل اوبدستان هند
سیراز قدح شرع بمستان هند
آنجاکه مجردان بهم بے نوشند
یک جرعه خویشتن پرستان هند

Gamble with your life. Take every chance you can.
You can't reach His union by talking.
They don't serve milk to drunks by the glass of sharia.*
In the place where wine is served,
They pour it only to those
Who have undressed from "self."
Not even a drop is given to those
Who worship themselves.
*Moral code and religious law associated with Islam

Canınla oyna, O'nun vuslatını masala vermezler sana.
Sarhoşlara, şeriat bardağıyla süt vermezler.
Şarabın sunulduğu yerde, şarap sadece kendinden
Soyunanlara verilir.
Kendine tapanlara, bir damlası bile verilmez.

155

Excellent advice for novices, and a repetition of the same theme Mevlana focuses on constantly: Unless you give up your self, you won't go anywhere.

78.

جان محرَم درگاه همی بايد بو د
دل پُر غم وپُرآه همی بايد بو د
ازخويش ماراه بيابی هركز
ازماسوی ماراه همی بايد بُود

Unless your soul has been intimate with this door
For a long time,
Unless your heart has been filled
With the pain and sorrows of Love,
You'll never find a road to us from your self.
You should give up your self and come to us from us.

Canın, uzun zaman o kapının mahremi olmadıkça,
Gönlün aşkın gamı ve ahıyla yanmadıkça, bize,
Kendinden yol bulamazsın.
Kendi varlığını verip, bizden bize yol alman gerek.

Very obvious. Love takes over everything.

79.

عشق ازازلست تا ابد خواهد بود
جبینك عشق عدد خواهد بود
فردا که قیامت آشکارا کردد
ای هرکه نه عاشق است رد خواهد بود

Love has no beginning, no end.
Love is eternal.
Countless people would search for it.
At the day of resurrection,
Everyone will be kicked off the Divine temple
Except lovers.

Aşkın ne başı vardır ne de sonu.
Aşk sonsuzdur.
Sayısız insanlar, Aşkı aramıştır.
Kıyamet gününde, Aşıklar dışında herkes,
Kutsal tapınaktan kovulacaklardır.

A rubai from the summit of the mountain.

80.

جشمى که نظر بذان کل و لا له کند
این کند جخ را براز ناله کند
مبها ی هزار ساله هرکز نکند
دیوانکئ که عش یکسا له کند

An eye that would see those roses, those tulips
Fills this whirling sky with wails and cries.
Intoxication that you can get from one-year-old Love
You couldn't get from a thousand-years-old wine.

Gülü ve lâleyi gören göz, şu dönüp
Duran gökyüzünü feryatlarla doldurur.
Bir yıllık aşkın yaptığı sarhoşluğu,
Bin yıllık şaraplar bile yapamaz.

Anybody who has been annihilated doesn't see the world, doesn't see soul; all they see is Love. They cannot deal with earthly problems. They cannot deal with eyes that—on the day of death—look at soul rather than Love.

81.

حاشا كه دل عشق جهان را نكرد
خود جيست بجز عشق كه اورا نكرد
بيزارسوم زچشم در روز ا جل
كز عشق دها كند كه جان را نكرد

Can a heart that has fallen in Love
Still look at the world? That is impossible!
In fact, there is nothing in the world to be seen
Besides Love.
I am tired and sick of the eyes that, on the day of death,
Look at soul instead of Love.

Gönül aşıkken nasıl hâlâ dünyaya bakabilir?
Hâşâ, bu olmaz.
Zaten bu dünyada, aşktan başka bakılacak ne vardır?
Ecel günü,
Aşkı bırakıp da can telaşına düşen gözden usanmışım.

This rubai smells of Shams.

82.

خاموش مرا زكفت كفنا رتوكرد
نے كارمرا حلاوت كا رتوكرد
بكریختم ازدام تو درخانۀ دل
دل دا مرشذ ومرا كرفنا رتوكرد

Be silent. Your words made me speechless.
Your sweetness made me soft and idle.
I ran from your traps to the house of my heart,
But the house of my heart became the trap for me.

Sus, sözlerin beni sözsüz etti.
İşinin tatlılığı, beni işsiz ve güçsüz bıraktı.
Tuzağından gönül evine kaçtım.
Ancak, bana gönlümün evi tuzak oldu.
Beni sana tutsak yaptı.

A rubai that focuses on suffering. Is Mevlana talking about Shams or God? Shams and God are often made interchangeable in Mevlana's poetry. This is a big statement: Shams becomes God; God becomes Shams. It's very common to put Shams in God's place. Many misunderstand the relationship between Melvana and Shams; it was not a romantic or sexual one. How could someone have a romantic or sexual relationship with God?

83.

خواهم كه دلم با غم تو خون باشد
كردست دهذ عمشرجه نيكو باشد
هان اى دلئ دل غم اودر بركير
تاجشم زنى خوذغم اوا واو باشد

I want to make my heart a friend to His troubles.
I want my heart to have plenty of His troubles.
Come to your senses, O lover.
Embrace His troubles, close your eyes.
When you open them,
You'll see that His troubles have become Him.

Gönlümün O'nun dertleriyle dost olmasını isterim.
Gönlümün O'nun dertleriyle dolmasını isterim.
Ey aşık, kendine gel, O'nun dertlerine sarıl ve gözlerini
kapa.
Gözlerini açtığında, göreceksin ki O'nun dertleri O olmuş.

167

Mevlana could be referring here to God or Shams. In any case, reason is downgraded into its proper place.

84.

How can the sun get the beauty of Your face?
The fastest wind can't reach
A single thread of Your hair.
Even reason, who is the king of the city of existence,
Becomes crazy when he reaches Your town.

Güneşte kim oluyor ki, Senin yüzünün
Güzelliğini elde etsin.
En şiddetli esen rüzgâr bile, kimdir ki saçının
Bir teline erişebilsin.
Varlık şehrinin sultanı olan akıl bile,
Senin mahallene gelince deli ve divâne olur.

Another earthly rubai from the bottom of the mountain.

85.

خون درِدل عاشقان جوحیحون کرد
عاشق حوکفی برسرآن خون کردذ
جسم تو جوآ سیا وآ بش عشقست
جون آب نباشذآ سیاجون کردذ

Blood boils in the hearts of the lovers,
Like the Jayhoun* river in the moutains.
Lovers are like foam over the whirling blood.
Your body resembles a millstone.
How could a millstone turn without water?
*A long South-Asian river; historical Latin name, Oxus; modern local
name, Amu Darya*

Kan, âşıkların gönüllerinden *Ceyhun gibi kaynar, coşar.
Âşıkta, o kanın üstünde bir köpük gibi döner.
Bedenin değirmene benzer, suyu âşktır.
Su olmayınca değirmen nasıl döner?
Orta Asya'daki amu- derya

Here, Mevlana is most likely referring to Shams. Mevlana is speaking from the middle of the mountain, when his annihilation is not complete, but still comes and goes. He is in Essence, though, and it is impossible for Essence to appear.

86.

داماں حلال توزد ستم نشوُد
سهاي توازد ماغ مستم نشوُد
كوبي نومراجناتك هستى نمِسا
كربنايم جناتك هستم نشوُد

I still hold the skirt of Your greatness.
The drunkenness from the wine You have served
Still remains in my head.
"Appear as you are," You told me.
But, it is impossible to appear as I am.

Ululuk eteğini elimden bırakmam. Bana
Ezelde sunduğun şarapların, sarhoş
Başımdan çıkmaz. Bana dedin ki:
"Nasılsan, kendini öyle göster."
Ancak, olduğum gibi görünsem, olmaz.

A clear description of Love that comes with annihilation as opposed to earthly, symbolic love.

87.

در عشق نه پستی نه بلندی باشد
نی هوشی نه هوشمندی باشد
قُرابی و سبحی و مریدی بود
قلّاشی و کم زنی و رندی باشد

In Love, no one is low, no one is high.
Neither sobriety nor drunkenness exist in Love.
There is no protector, no sheikh, no disciple in Love,
Only poverty.
Kalanderi* rinds† are in Love.
*A group of dervishes
†A jolly, unconventional mystic; certain type of Sufi

Aşkta ne alçaklık vardır, ne yükseklik…
Ne kendinden geçiş vardır, ne aklı başında olmak.
Aşta hafızlık, şeyhlik ve müritlik yoktur.
Âşkta sadece yokluk, hiçlik, kalenderlik* rindlik† vardır.
*Dünyadan vazgeçmiş derviş
†Neşeli, alışılmadık mistik kişi

Soul means nothing in *fanâ* [annihilation]. Soul is an earthly word. We have no idea about our body; we have no idea about our soul. But, Love is something else. After *fanâ*, Love comes and crushes everything earthly. Your body, your soul, your worth, your everything is gone.

88.

دراعشق هزارجان ودل بس نكسد
جان خودجه محل حديث جان كو نكى
اين راه كسى رود كه درهر قدمى
صدجان بدهد كه روى وابس نكند

To sacrifice thousands of hearts and souls for Love
Is not enough!
What is soul? It isn't even worth being mentioned!
One who goes on the way of Love
Must sacrifice hundreds of souls at every step
And never look back.

Aşka binlerce can ve gönül verilse bile yine yetmez.
Can da nedir ki? Yeri mi var canın?
Sözü bile edilemez.
Aşk yolunda giden kişi, her adımda yüzlerce can verir,
Ve arkasına bakmadan gider.

Mevlana could be talking about God's door or Shams's door. Lovers come to the door, stay there awhile, then leave. But, Mevlana stays there forever.

89.

در کوی تو عاشقان فرا اینده ورند
خون جکرازدیده کشا یندور ند
من بر تو مقیم باذا مجاك
ودنی دکران جو باذا آیند ورند

Lovers gather at Your quarter, but later they leave.
They shed bloody tears, wail, and then they leave.
I am like dust on Your door and stay there forever,
While others come and go like the wind.

Mahallende âşıklar toplanır, sonra da giderler.
Onlar, gözlerinden kanlı yaşlar dökerler ve sonra
Seni bırakıp giderler.
Ben, toprak gibi her zaman senin kapındayım.
Başkaları gibi değilim.
Onlar yel gibi gelip, yel gibi giderler.

Anybody who goes through *fanâ* [annihilation] realizes that when a person reaches beyond the earth, Love comes in and crushes everything in the earth. Nothing remains. No good, no bad, no high, no low, no black, no white. Nothing remains. They have reached non-dualistic perception.

90.

دریخزفلک جو عشق جوجا کبرد
نا عرش هم فتنه وغوغا کبرد
جون روح شود جهان نه بالاونه زیر
جون عشق تو روح راز بالا کبرد

When Your Love takes its place
In the mind of the firmament,
Trouble fills the world and reaches the sky.
When Your Love catches the world's soul,
The world turns into one soul,
And neither up nor down remains.

Senin Aşkın, feleğin aklında yer bulunca,
Arşa kadar bütün alemi fitneler kaplar,
Kavgalarla dolar âlem.
Aşkın, dünyanın ruhunu yakalayınca,
Dünya tek ruha döner, artık ne yukarı
Kalır ne de aşağı.

One doesn't dive into the river of life to find a pearl. The one who dives into the river of life is the one who stays there, who dies there. Mortality comes from earthly things; immortality comes from getting earthly things out of yourself.

91.

دُر می طلبی نجشه دُر بر ناید
جوينك دُر بقعر دريا بايد
ابن كوهر قيمتی كسی راشايد
كزآب حيات تشنه بیرون آید

Don't search for a pearl in the river.
You have to dive to the bottom of the ocean of Truth.
The only one who deserves this pearl
Is the one who finds it
And isn't thirsty for the river of life.

İnciyi ırmakta arama, çünkü bulamazsın.
İnciyi bulmak için hakikat denizinin dibine dalmalısın.
Bu inci bengisuya dalıp da hâlâ susuz kalanındır.

The same message as in the previous rubai.

92.

دری داری که بحر را پُردار د
دُری که هزا بحر پُر دری دآر د
خواهی که بیا سی فروانی نجنُر
زان روی که حر روی بآخر دآرد

You have a pearl that fills thousands of oceans.
If you want to find it, don't be silly:
If you follow an ass, you'll end up in a barn.
Look instead inside of your heart.

Sende bir inci var ki, denizleri doldurur.
O'nu bulmak istiyorsan, eşeklikten vazgeçip
Kendi içine dal.
Eşekçesine gidersen, sadece ahıra varırsın.

Very obvious.

93.

دررُوزه جوازطبع دى باكْ شُوى
اندرى پاكان تو براقلك شُوَ
ازسوزِش روزه نوركردى تومجوع
ورْظلمت اقمه لقمه خاكْ شُوى

You will be purified from bad habits by fasting.
You will follow the attained ascent to the sky by fasting.
You will be burned like a candle by the fire of fasting.
Become divine light. The darkness of a bite
Makes you a morsel for the ground.

Oruçla kötü huylarından arınırsın.
Ermiş kişilerin peşine düşüp göklere yükselirsin.
Orucun mânâ ateşiyle mum gibi yanar, nur olursun.
Lokmanın karanlığı seni toprağa lokma yapar.

Human time is divided into half day, half night. Mevlana considers both of them to be lame donkeys. Once somebody breaks the cycle, gets out of time and place, day and night disappear.

94.

دولآ مذوغوغای تودربربردارذ
شب آمذوسودای تودرسردارذ
كارشب وروزنیست ابن كارمنست
كی دوخرلنک بارمن بردارذ

Day brought me Your troubles and fights.
Night filled my head with Your Love.
But all this is not the business of day or night;
This is my business.
How could those two lame donkeys carry my load?

Gün, senin kavganı ve gürültünü getirdi.
Gece, başımı senin âşkınla doldurdu.
Bu, geceyle gündüzün işi değildir.
Bu, benim işimdir.
İki topal eşek, nasıl benim yükümü taşıyabilir?

189

Yes. Fasting.

95.

دوزه محک محتشم و دون آمذ
ذنهار مکوجون که ز بیجون آمذ
دوز بست که از وذای کردون آمذ
نان روز بهی که ر وذافزون آمذ

Fasting is the touchstone of good and bad.
Don't ask me how that could be:
This came from the One who is beyond questions.
Fasting is the divine food
That comes from beyond the sky.
It makes everything better, including you.

Oruç, iyinin ve kötünün mihenk taşıdır.
Sakın bu nasıl olur deme.
Bu, soruların ötesinde olandan geldi.
Oruç, bir gök sofrasıdır.
O sofraya oturduğun için günahlardan temizlenip,
Iyi bir hale geldin.

191

The Sultan and his *Vizier* [secretary] who keeps the *Divan* [anthology] represent humans. When someone reaches *fanâ* [annihilation], their exuberance makes them crazy, so much so that the messages they get would be impossible for a human to write down.

96.

روزی که مرا عشق بو دیوانه کند
دیوانکی کنم که دیوان نکند
حکم قلم بوآن کند با دل من
کز نوک قلم خواجه دیوان نکند

When Your Love makes me crazy,
I will do things that even the devil won't do.
Your eyelashes write such messages on my heart
That the Vizier of the Sultan's Divan can't write them.

Aşkın, beni deli divane ettiği gün, öylesine delilikler
Edeceğim ki şeytanlar ve periler bile o delilikleri edemez.
Kipriklerin gönlüme öyle yazılar yazdı ki,
Sultanın divanında vezir bile o yazıları yazamaz.

Just like in *all* religions that follow one particular messenger, most Christians say there is no one in the world like Jesus. But, people don't see everyone on earth: There are actually hundreds in the world like Jesus; people just can't see them.

97.

Don't ever say,
"No one walks towards the Truth nowadays.
No one is like Jesus, like a concealed saint in our time."
Since you are not intimate with the secrets of the path,
You are assuming that everyone else is ignorant, too.

Sakın "Hak yoluna, itlak yoluna gidenlere artık
Yoktur" deme.
İzlerinin tozları belirmeyen İsa huylular günümüzde
Yok diye söyleme.
Sen sırları bilmediğin için, başkalarını da yok sanıyorsun.

Ecstacy is the sign of *fanâ* [annihilation]. Mevlana is comparing this existence with non-existence [*fanâ*].

98.

شب کردم گرد شهر چون باد و خواب
از کشیدن گرد شهر کسی با بیخواب
عقلست که چیزها را موضع جوید
تمیز و ادب مجو یو از مست و خراب

At night, I turned around the city like wind,
Running like water.
How can sleep overcome the one
Who walks around the city in darkness?
Mind is the one who wants to have everything in order.
Don't ask for reason or manners from the drunk.

Gece şehrin etrafında rüzgâr gibi estim, su
Gece karanlıkta şehirde yürüyeni nasıl uyku tutar?
Her şeyin düzenli olmasını sadece akıl ister.
Sarhoştan, ne sebep sor, ne de üslûp bekle.

Mevlana focuses on this idea in any number of his rubais. Existence turns into Absence, Absence into existence every moment, all the time, but, this reality is beyond our human perception. In one instance, Mevlana says that hundreds of caravans are coming from nowhere, coming into existence, then turning back again, but it happens so fast, we just don't see it.

99.

عشقی آمذ که عشقها سودا شد
سوزیدم وخاکستم هم لا شد
بازازهوس سوز توخاکستم
واکنت هزار بارصورتها شد

When this Love came, all other loves disappeared.
I was burned, turned into ashes.
Those ashes were scattered and disappeared.
Then, with Your help, they came back
And formed thousands of shapes again.

Öyle bir Âşk geldi ki bütün aşklar,
O'nun yanında yok oldu.
Ben, yandım ve kül oldum.
Külüm de savruldu, yok oldu.
Derken yine Senin havana kapılıp külüm
Geri geldi ve binlerce şekillere büründüm.

This rubai is from the summit of the mountain. At the summit, you don't feel anything about the earth. No good, no bad, no black, no white, no God, no creatures. You don't feel anything.

100.

جز درمدمنه عشق تو در کوش نماند
جانرازحلاوت ازل هوس نماند
بی رنگی عشق رنگها به آمیخت
ورحالت بی رنگ فراموس نماند

There is nothing remaining in my ears
But Love's murmur.
There is nothing remaining in my soul—
No reason, no thought—
Only the sweetness of Eternity.
The colorless brush of Love mixed all colors;
Now, it can't remember its past.

Kulağımda Senin aşk gürültünden başka hiçbir şey kalmadı.
Canımda ezel tatlılığından başka ne akıl, ne de fikir kaldı.
Aşkın renksizliği, renklerle karıştığı için
Renksiz halini bile hatırlamıyor.

The Sources

Between 1992 and 2003, Ergin translated Mevlana's entire *Dîvân-i Kebîr* from Turkish into English. This *Dîvân* contains Mevlana's longer poems [gazels]. In total, the translation includes 44,000 verses published in 22 volumes. The *Dîvân* also contains 2,217 short verses [rubais] which Ergin translated and compiled under the title, the *Rubâîlar of Rumi*. The selections in *Unknown Rumi* comprise 100 of those short verses

Abdulbaki Gölpinarli

Ergin based his English translations on the works of the Turkish scholar Abdulbaki Gölpinarli (d.1982). Gölpinarli used four sources for his Turkish translation of the original Persian (Farsi):

1.   Two volumes of the *Dîvân* which were compiled between July 2, 1367 and October 13, 1368 by Hasan ibni Osman-al Mavlavi. It is registered at the Mevlana Museum in Konya as No. 68 and No. 69. This is considered to be the most reliable *Dîvân* available today. Mevlana died in 1273, and it was less than 100 years later that this copy was made.
2.   The *Dîvân* registered at the Library of the University of Istanbul, No. 334, which was compiled in the 15th century.
3.   The *Dîvân* owned by Gölpinarli, prepared in 1691 in Baghdad. Later, this *Dîvân* was donated to the Mevlana Museum in Konya.
4.   Eight volumes of *Kulliyât-é shams yâ dîwân-é kabîr-e mawlânâ jalâluddîn Muhammad mashhûr ba-mawlawî* prepared by Badî'uzzamân Forûzânfar in 1965.

Hasan ibni Osman-al Mavlavi

For preparing the translations of the rubais of Rumi, Ergin had 35 mm photographs taken of the entire *Dîvân-i Kebîr* compiled by Hasan ibni Osman-al Mavlavi, mentioned above. As a result, Ergin has been able to present each rubai in the Persian exactly as recorded by Osman-al Mavlavi, followed by Gölpinarli's Turkish translation of the Persian and Ergin's English translation of the Turkish.

An Additional Challenge

It should be noted that Ergin consulted with several Persian scholars to address the challenge of not being able to translate directly from the original language, but from a second language into a third.

Notes

There frequently seems to be controversy as to the authenticity of translations, especially in regards to translations of the works of figures as important as Mevlana. The references below are the original Turkish sources used for the translations presented in this book. Also included is the page number from the *Rubâîlar of Rumi* from which these selections were taken.

In the Introduction

1. Ergin, *Dîvân-i Kabîr Meter 9*, 177, v.1103-1110.
2. Can, *Hz. Mevlânâ'nin Rubâîleri*, v. 1042; Ergin, *Rubâîlar of Rumi*, 257, v. 1; Forûzânfar (ed.), *Kulliyât-é shams yâ dîwân-é kabîr-e mawlânâ jalâluddîn Muhammad mashhûr ba-mawlawî*, v. 1173; Gölpinarli, *Mevlânâ Celâleddin, Rubâîler*, D2(274), v. 131-1.

In the Rubais

Selection
Number

1. Can, *Hz. Mevlânâ'nin Rubâîleri*, v. 821; Ergin, *Rubâîlar of Rumi*, 197, v. 1; Forûzânfar (ed.), *Kulliyât-é shams yâ dîwân-é kabîr-e mawlânâ jalâluddîn Muhammad mashhûr ba-mawlawî*, v. 768; Gölpinarli, *Mevlânâ Celâleddin, Rubâîler*, D91, v. 206.
2. Can, *Hz. Mevlânâ'nin Rubâîleri*, v. 20; Ergin, *Rubâîlar of Rumi*, 10, v. 3; Forûzânfar (ed.), *Kulliyât-é shams yâ dîwân-é kabîr-e mawlânâ jalâluddîn Muhammad mashhûr ba-mawlawî*, v. 20; Gölpinarli, *Mevlânâ Celâleddin, Rubâîler*, A16, v. 7.
3.` Can, *Hz. Mevlânâ'nin Rubâîleri*, v. 52; Ergin, *Rubâîlar of Rumi*, 16, v. 2; Forûzânfar (ed.), *Kulliyât-é shams yâ dîwân-é kabîr-e mawlânâ jalâluddîn Muhammad mashhûr ba-mawlawî*, v. 52; Gölpinarli, *Mevlânâ Celâleddin, Rubâîler*, A22, v. 56.
4. Can, *Hz. Mevlânâ'nin Rubâîleri*, v. 23; Ergin, *Rubâîlar of Rumi*, 17, v. 1; Forûzânfar (ed.), *Kulliyât-é shams yâ dîwân-é kabîr-e mawlânâ jalâluddîn Muhammad mashhûr ba-mawlawî*, v. 23; Gölpinarli, *Mevlânâ Celâleddin, Rubâîler*, A17, v.21.
5. Can, *Hz. Mevlânâ'nin Rubâîleri*, v. 5; Ergin, *Rubâîlar of Rumi*, 20, v 2; Forûzânfar (ed.), *Kulliyât-é shams yâ dîwân-é kabîr-e mawlânâ jalâluddîn Muhammad mashhûr ba-mawlawî*, v. 5; Gölpinarli,

Mevlânâ Celâleddin, Rubâîler, A18, v. 27.

6. Can, *Hz. Mevlânâ'nin Rubâîleri,* v. 16; Ergin, *Rubâîlar of Rumi,* 22, v. 4; Forûzânfar (ed.), *Kulliyât-é shams yâ dîwân-é kabîr-e mawlânâ jalâluddîn Muhammad mashhûr ba-mawlawî,* v. 16; Gölpinarli, *Mevlânâ Celâleddin, Rubâîler,* A23, v. 65.

7. Can, *Hz. Mevlânâ'nin Rubâîleri,* v. 70; Ergin, *Rubâîlar of Rumi,* 23, v. 2; Forûzânfar (ed.), *Kulliyât-é shams yâ dîwân-é kabîr-e mawlânâ jalâluddîn Muhammad mashhûr ba-mawlawî,* v. 70; Gölpinarli, *Mevlânâ Celâleddin, Rubâîler,* A19, v. 35.

8. Can, *Hz. Mevlânâ'nin Rubâîleri,* v. 15; Ergin, *Rubâîlar of Rumi,* 24, v. 4; Forûzânfar (ed.), *Kulliyât-é shams yâ dîwân-é kabîr-e mawlânâ jalâluddîn Muhammad mashhûr ba-mawlawî,* v. 15; Gölpinarli, *Mevlânâ Celâleddin, Rubâîler,* A, --.

9. Can, *Hz. Mevlânâ'nin Rubâîleri,* v. 95; Ergin, *Rubâîlar of Rumi,* 29, v. 4; Forûzânfar (ed.), *Kulliyât-é shams yâ dîwân-é kabîr-e mawlânâ jalâluddîn Muhammad mashhûr ba-mawlawî,* v. 82; Gölpinarli, *Mevlânâ Celâleddin, Rubâîler,* B25, v. 11.

10. Can, *Hz. Mevlânâ'nin Rubâîleri,* v. 193; Ergin, *Rubâîlar of Rumi,* 36, v. 2; Forûzânfar (ed.), *Kulliyât-é shams yâ dîwân-é kabîr-e mawlânâ jalâluddîn Muhammad mashhûr ba-mawlawî,* v. 175; Gölpinarli, *Mevlânâ Celâleddin, Rubâîler,* T49, v. 181.

11. Can, *Hz. Mevlânâ'nin Rubâîleri,* v. 200; Ergin, *Rubâîlar of Rumi,* 38, v. 1; Forûzânfar (ed.), *Kulliyât-é shams yâ dîwân-é kabîr-e mawlânâ jalâluddîn Muhammad mashhûr ba-mawlawî,* v. 182; Gölpinarli, *Mevlânâ Celâleddin, Rubâîler,* T29, v. 14.

12. Can, *Hz. Mevlânâ'nin Rubâîleri,* v. 370; Ergin, *Rubâîlar of Rumi,* 40, v. 4; Forûzânfar (ed.), *Kulliyât-é shams yâ dîwân-é kabîr-e mawlânâ jalâluddîn Muhammad mashhûr ba-mawlawî,* v. 352; Gölpinarli, *Mevlânâ Celâleddin, Rubâîler,* T51, v. 192.

13. Can, *Hz. Mevlânâ'nin Rubâîleri,* v. 413; Ergin, *Rubâîlar of Rumi,* 44, v. 1; Forûzânfar (ed.), *Kulliyât-é shams yâ dîwân-é kabîr-e mawlânâ jalâluddîn Muhammad mashhûr ba-mawlawî,* v. 395; Gölpinarli, *Mevlânâ Celâleddin, Rubâîler,* T28, v. 3.

14. Can, *Hz. Mevlânâ'nin Rubâîleri,* v. 124; Ergin, *Rubâîlar of Rumi,* 44, v. 2; Forûzânfar (ed.), *Kulliyât-é shams yâ dîwân-é kabîr-e mawlânâ jalâluddîn Muhammad mashhûr ba-mawlawî,* v. 106; Gölpinarli, *Mevlânâ Celâleddin, Rubâîler,* T48, v. 166.

15. Can, *Hz. Mevlânâ'nin Rubâîleri,* v. 203; Ergin, *Rubâîlar of Rumi,* 45,

v. 4; Forûzânfar (ed.), *Kulliyât-é shams yâ dîwân-é kabîr-e mawlânâ jalâluddîn Muhammad mashhûr ba-mawlawî*, v. 185; Gölpinarli, *Mevlânâ Celâleddin, Rubâîler*, T48, v. 170.

16. Can, *Hz. Mevlânâ'nin Rubâîleri*, v. 339; Ergin, *Rubâîlar of Rumi*, 47, v. 4; Forûzânfar (ed.), *Kulliyât-é shams yâ dîwân-é kabîr-e mawlânâ jalâluddîn Muhammad mashhûr ba-mawlawî*, v. 321; Gölpinarli, *Mevlânâ Celâleddin, Rubâîler*, T29, v. 13.

17. Can, *Hz. Mevlânâ'nin Rubâîleri*, v. 327; Ergin, *Rubâîlar of Rumi*, 49, v. 4; Forûzânfar (ed.), *Kulliyât-é shams yâ dîwân-é kabîr-e mawlânâ jalâluddîn Muhammad mashhûr ba-mawlawî*, v. 309; Gölpinarli, *Mevlânâ Celâleddin, Rubâîler*, T32, v.38.

18. Can, *Hz. Mevlânâ'nin Rubâîleri*, v. 406; Ergin, *Rubâîlar of Rumi*, 51, v. 1; Forûzânfar (ed.), *Kulliyât-é shams yâ dîwân-é kabîr-e mawlânâ jalâluddîn Muhammad mashhûr ba-mawlawî*, v. 388; Gölpinarli, *Mevlânâ Celâleddin, Rubâîler*, T33, v. 43.

19. Can, *Hz. Mevlânâ'nin Rubâîleri*, v. 329; Ergin, *Rubâîlar of Rumi*, 52, v.1; Forûzânfar (ed.), *Kulliyât-é shams yâ dîwân-é kabîr-e mawlânâ jalâluddîn Muhammad mashhûr ba-mawlawî*, v. 311; Gölpinarli, *Mevlânâ Celâleddin, Rubâîler*, T32, v. 37.

20. Can, *Hz. Mevlânâ'nin Rubâîleri*, v. 388; Ergin, *Rubâîlar of Rumi*, 57, v. 1; Forûzânfar (ed.), *Kulliyât-é shams yâ dîwân-é kabîr-e mawlânâ jalâluddîn Muhammad mashhûr ba-mawlawî*, v. 371; Gölpinarli, *Mevlânâ Celâleddin, Rubâîler*, T31, v. 31.

21. Can, *Hz. Mevlânâ'nin Rubâîleri*, v. 337; Ergin, *Rubâîlar of Rumi*, 64, v. 3; Forûzânfar (ed.), *Kulliyât-é shams yâ dîwân-é kabîr-e mawlânâ jalâluddîn Muhammad mashhûr ba-mawlawî*, v. 319; Gölpinarli, *Mevlânâ Celâleddin, Rubâîler*, T34, v. 58.

22. Can, *Hz. Mevlânâ'nin Rubâîleri*, v. 152; Ergin, *Rubâîlar of Rumi*, 65, v. 2; Forûzânfar (ed.), *Kulliyât-é shams yâ dîwân-é kabîr-e mawlânâ jalâluddîn Muhammad mashhûr ba-mawlawî*, v. 134; Gölpinarli, *Mevlânâ Celâleddin, Rubâîler*, T56, v. 237.

23. Can, *Hz. Mevlânâ'nin Rubâîleri*, v. 412; Ergin, *Rubâîlar of Rumi*, 65, v. 3; Forûzânfar (ed.), *Kulliyât-é shams yâ dîwân-é kabîr-e mawlânâ jalâluddîn Muhammad mashhûr ba-mawlawî*, v. 394; Gölpinarli, *Mevlânâ Celâleddin, Rubâîler*, T56, v. 236.

24. Can, *Hz. Mevlânâ'nin Rubâîleri*, v. 268; Ergin, *Rubâîlar of Rumi*, 68, v. 3; Forûzânfar (ed.), *Kulliyât-é shams yâ dîwân-é kabîr-e mawlânâ jalâluddîn Muhammad mashhûr ba-mawlawî*, v. 250; Gölpinarli,

Mevlânâ Celâleddin, Rubâîler, T35, v. 61.

25. Can, *Hz. Mevlânâ'nin Rubâîleri,* v. 328; Ergin, *Rubâîlar of Rumi,* 69, v. 1; Forûzânfar (ed.), *Kulliyât-é shams yâ dîwân-é kabîr-e mawlânâ jalâluddîn Muhammad mashhûr ba-mawlawî,* v. 310; Gölpinarli, *Mevlânâ Celâleddin, Rubâîler,* T56, v. 240.

26. Can, *Hz. Mevlânâ'nin Rubâîleri,* v. 429; Ergin, *Rubâîlar of Rumi,* 69, v. 2; Forûzânfar (ed.), *Kulliyât-é shams yâ dîwân-é kabîr-e mawlânâ jalâluddîn Muhammad mashhûr ba-mawlawî,* v. 411; Gölpinarli, *Mevlânâ Celâleddin, Rubâîler,* T56, v. 238.

27. Can, *Hz. Mevlânâ'nin Rubâîleri,* v. 194; Ergin, *Rubâîlar of Rumi,* 69, v. 4; Forûzânfar (ed.), *Kulliyât-é shams yâ dîwân-é kabîr-e mawlânâ jalâluddîn Muhammad mashhûr ba-mawlawî,* v. 176; Gölpinarli, *Mevlânâ Celâleddin, Rubâîler,* T35, v. 66.

28. Can, *Hz. Mevlânâ'nin Rubâîleri,* v. 345; Ergin, *Rubâîlar of Rumi,* 70, v. 4; Forûzânfar (ed.), *Kulliyât-é shams yâ dîwân-é kabîr-e mawlânâ jalâluddîn Muhammad mashhûr ba-mawlawî,* v. 327; Gölpinarli, *Mevlânâ Celâleddin, Rubâîler,* T36, v. 69.

29. Can, *Hz. Mevlânâ'nin Rubâîleri,* v. 1605; Ergin, *Rubâîlar of Rumi,* 335, v. 2; Forûzânfar (ed.), *Kulliyât-é shams yâ dîwân-é kabîr-e mawlânâ jalâluddîn Muhammad mashhûr ba-mawlawî,* v. 1442; Gölpinarli, *Mevlânâ Celâleddin, Rubâîler,* N269, v. 18.

30. Can, *Hz. Mevlânâ'nin Rubâîleri,* v. 410; Ergin, *Rubâîlar of Rumi,* 74, v. 4; Forûzânfar (ed.), *Kulliyât-é shams yâ dîwân-é kabîr-e mawlânâ jalâluddîn Muhammadâ mashhûr ba-mawlawî,* v. 392; Gölpinarli, *Mevlânâ Celâleddin, Rubâîler,* T57, v. 248.

31. Can, *Hz. Mevlânâ'nin Rubâîleri,* v. 322; Ergin, *Rubâîlar of Rumi,* 76, v. 3; Forûzânfar (ed.), *Kulliyât-é shams yâ dîwân-é kabîr-e mawlânâ jalâluddîn Muhammad mashhûr ba-mawlawî,* v. 304; Gölpinarli, *Mevlânâ Celâleddin, Rubâîler,* T37, v. 83.

32. Can, *Hz. Mevlânâ'nin Rubâîleri,* v. 244; Ergin, *Rubâîlar of Rumi,* 80, v. 1; Forûzânfar (ed.), *Kulliyât-é shams yâ dîwân-é kabîr-e mawlânâ jalâluddîn Muhammad mashhûr ba-mawlawî,* v. 226; Gölpinarli, *Mevlânâ Celâleddin, Rubâîler,* T(261) 38, v. 89.

33. Can, *Hz. Mevlânâ'nin Rubâîleri,* v. 306; Ergin, *Rubâîlar of Rumi,* 80, v. 4; Forûzânfar (ed.), *Kulliyât-é shams yâ dîwân-é kabîr-e mawlânâ jalâluddîn Muhammad mashhûr ba-mawlawî,* v. 288; Gölpinarli, *Mevlânâ Celâleddin, Rubâîler,* T38, v. 87.

34. Can, *Hz. Mevlânâ'nin Rubâîleri,* v. 443; Ergin, *Rubâîlar of Rumi,* 82,

v. 1; Forûzânfar (ed.), *Kulliyât-é shams yâ dîwân-é kabîr-e mawlânâ jalâluddîn Muhammad mashhûr ba-mawlawî*, v. 425; Gölpinarli, *Mevlânâ Celâleddin, Rubâîler*, T39, v. 96.

35. Can, *Hz. Mevlânâ'nin Rubâîleri*, v. 385; Ergin, *Rubâîlar of Rumi*, 89, v. 1; Forûzânfar (ed.), *Kulliyât-é shams yâ dîwân-é kabîr-e mawlânâ jalâluddîn Muhammad mashhûr ba-mawlawî*, v. 367; Gölpinarli, *Mevlânâ Celâleddin, Rubâîler*, T40, v. 107.

36. Can, *Hz. Mevlânâ'nin Rubâîleri*, v. 409; Ergin, *Rubâîlar of Rumi*, 90, v. 1; Forûzânfar (ed.), *Kulliyât-é shams yâ dîwân-é kabîr-e mawlânâ jalâluddîn Muhammad mashhûr ba-mawlawî*, v. 391; Gölpinarli, *Mevlânâ Celâleddin, Rubâîler*, T61, v. 275.

37. Can, *Hz. Mevlânâ'nin Rubâîleri*, v. 130; Ergin, *Rubâîlar of Rumi*, 92, v. 4; Forûzânfar (ed.), *Kulliyât-é shams yâ dîwân-é kabîr-e mawlânâ jalâluddîn Muhammad mashhûr ba-mawlawî*, v. 112; Gölpinarli, *Mevlânâ Celâleddin, Rubâîler*, T50, v. 183.

38. Can, *Hz. Mevlânâ'nin Rubâîleri*, v. 431; Ergin, *Rubâîlar of Rumi*, 93, v. 3; Forûzânfar (ed.), *Kulliyât-é shams yâ dîwân-é kabîr-e mawlânâ jalâluddîn Muhammad mashhûr ba-mawlawî*, v. 413; Gölpinarli, *Mevlânâ Celâleddin, Rubâîler*, T42, v. 118.

39. Can, *Hz. Mevlânâ'nin Rubâîleri*, v. 153; Ergin, *Rubâîlar of Rumi*, 94, v.1; Forûzânfar (ed.), *Kulliyât-é shams yâ dîwân-é kabîr-e mawlânâ jalâluddîn Muhammad mashhûr ba-mawlawî*, v. 135; Gölpinarli, *Mevlânâ Celâleddin, Rubâîler*, T61, v. 282.

40. Can, *Hz. Mevlânâ'nin Rubâîleri*, v. 428; Ergin, *Rubâîlar of Rumi*, 95, v. 2; Forûzânfar (ed.), *Kulliyât-é shams yâ dîwân-é kabîr-e mawlânâ jalâluddîn Muhammad mashhûr ba-mawlawî*, v. 410; Gölpinarli, *Mevânâ Celâleddin, Rubâîler*, T42, v. 124.

41. Can, *Hz. Mevlânâ'nin Rubâîleri*, v. 414; Ergin, *Rubâîlar of Rumi*, 96, v. 3; Forûzânfar (ed.), *Kulliyât-é shams yâ dîwân-é kabîr-e mawlânâ jalâluddîn Muhammad mashhûr ba-mawlawî*, v. 396; Gölpinarli, *Mevlânâ Celâleddin, Rubâîler*, T42, v. 125.

42. Can, *Hz. Mevlânâ'nin Rubâîleri*, v. 390; Ergin, *Rubâîlar of Rumi*, 97, v. 2; Forûzânfar (ed.), *Kulliyât-é shams yâ dîwân-é kabîr-e mawlânâ jalâluddîn Muhammad mashhûr ba-mawlawî*, v. 372; Gölpinarli, *Mevlânâ Celâleddin, Rubâîler*, T43, v. 128.

43. Can, *Hz. Mevlânâ'nin Rubâîleri*, v. 156; Ergin, *Rubâîlar of Rumi*, 100, v. 1; *Forûzânfar (ed.), Kulliyât-é shams yâ dîwân-é kabîr-e mawlânâ jalâluddîn Muhammad mashhûr ba-mawlawî*, v. 138;

Gölpinarli, *Mevlânâ Celâleddin, Rubâîler,* T63-292.

44. Can, *Hz. Mevlânâ'nin Rubâîleri,* v. 123; Ergin, *Rubâîlar of Rumi,* 103, v. 3; Forûzânfar (ed.), *Kulliyât-é shams yâ dîwân-é kabîr-e mawlânâ jalâluddîn Muhammad mashhûr ba-mawlawî,* v. 105; Gölpinarli, *Mevlânâ Celâleddin, Rubâîler,* T44, v. 138.

45. Can, *Hz. Mevlânâ'nin Rubâîleri,* v. 257; Ergin, *Rubâîlar of Rumi,* 105, v. 2; Forûzânfar (ed.), *Kulliyât-é shams yâ dîwân-é kabîr-e mawlânâ jalâluddîn Muhammad mashhûr ba-mawlawî,* v. 239; Gölpinarli, *Mevlânâ Celâleddin, Rubâîler,* T64, v. 304.

46. Can, *Hz. Mevlânâ'nin Rubâîleri,* v. 225; Ergin, *Rubâîlar of Rumi,* 107, v. 2; Forûzânfar (ed.), *Kulliyât-é shams yâ dîwân-é kabîr-e mawlânâ jalâluddîn Muhammad mashhûr ba-mawlawî,* v. 207; Gölpinarli, *Mevlânâ Celâleddin, Rubâîler,* T45, v. 144.

47. Can, *Hz. Mevlânâ'nin Rubâîleri,* v. 434; Ergin, *Rubâîlar of Rumi,*109, v. 3; Forûzânfar (ed.), *Kulliyât-é shams yâ dîwân-é kabîr-e mawlânâ jalâluddîn Muhammad mashhûr ba-mawlawî,* v. 416; Gölpinarli, *Mevlânâ Celâleddin, Rubâîler,* T65, v. 310.

48. Can, *Hz. Mevlânâ'nin Rubâîleri,* v. 304; Ergin, *Rubâîlar of Rumi,* 113, v. 2; Forûzânfar (ed.), *Kulliyât-é shams yâ dîwân-é kabîr-e mawlânâ jalâluddîn Muhammad mashhûr ba-mawlawî,* v. 286; Gölpinarli, *Mevlânâ Celâleddin, Rubâîler,* T65, v. 316.

49. Can, *Hz. Mevlânâ'nin Rubâîleri,* v. 362; Ergin, *Rubâîlar of Rumi,*114, v. 2; Forûzânfar (ed.), *Kulliyât-é shams yâ dîwân-é kabîr-e mawlânâ jalâluddîn Muhammad mashhûr ba-mawlawî,* v. 344; Gölpinarli, *Mevlânâ Celâleddin, Rubâîler,* T65, v. 315.

50. Can, *Hz. Mevlânâ'nin Rubâîleri,* v. 382; Ergin, *Rubâîlar of Rumi,* 115, v. 4; Forûzânfar (ed.), *Kulliyât-é shams yâ dîwân-é kabîr-e mawlânâ jalâluddîn Muhammad mashhûr ba-mawlawî,* v. 364; Gölpinarli, *Mevlânâ Celâleddin, Rubâîler,* T47, v. 161.

51. Can, *Hz. Mevlânâ'nin Rubâîleri,* v. 371; Ergin, *Rubâîlar of Rumi,* 116, v. 3; Forûzânfar (ed.), *Kulliyât-é shams yâ dîwân-é kabîr-e mawlânâ jalâluddîn Muhammad mashhûr ba-mawlawî,* v. 353; Gölpinarli, *Mevlânâ Celâleddin, Rubâîler,* T66, v. 324.

52. Can, *Hz. Mevlânâ'nin Rubâîleri,* v. 487; Ergin, *Rubâîlar of Rumi,* 117, v. 2; Forûzânfar (ed.), *Kulliyât-é shams yâ dîwân-é kabîr-e mawlânâ jalâluddîn Muhammad mashhûr ba-mawlawî,* v. 432; Gölpinarli, *Mevlânâ Celâleddin, Rubâîler,* H1 67, v. 2.

53. Can, *Hz. Mevlânâ'nin Rubâîleri,* v. 772; Ergin, *Rubâîlar of Rumi,*

118, v. 1; Forûzânfar (ed.), *Kulliyât-é shams yâ dîwân-é kabîr-e mawlânâ jalâluddîn Muhammad mashhûr ba-mawlawî*, v. 718; Gölpinarli, *Mevlânâ Celâleddin, Rubâîler*, D69, v. 18.

54. Can, *Hz. Mevlânâ'nin Rubâîleri*, v. 713; Ergin, *Rubâîlar of Rumi*, 120, v. 3; Forûzânfar (ed.), *Kulliyât-é shams yâ dîwân-é kabîr-e mawlânâ jalâluddîn Muhammad mashhûr ba-mawlawî*, v. 659; Gölpinarli, *Mevlânâ Celâleddin, Rubâîler*, S69, v. 16.

55. Can, *Hz. Mevlânâ'nin Rubâîleri*, v. 714; Ergin, *Rubâîlar of Rumi*, 123, v. 2; Forûzânfar (ed.), *Kulliyât-é shams yâ dîwân-é kabîr-e mawlânâ jalâluddîn Muhammad mashhûr ba-mawlawî*, v. 660; Gölpinarli, *Mevlânâ Celâleddin, Rubâîler*, D69, v. 15.

56. Can, *Hz. Mevlânâ'nin Rubâîleri*, v. 558; Ergin, *Rubâîlar of Rumi*, 125, v. 2; Forûzânfar (ed.), *Kulliyât-é shams yâ dîwân-é kabîr-e mawlânâ jalâluddîn Muhammad mashhûr ba-mawlawî*, v. 533; Gölpinarli, *Mevlânâ Celâleddin, Rubâîler*, D80, v. 110.

57. Can, *Hz. Mevlânâ'nin Rubâîleri*, v. 561; Ergin, *Rubâîlar of Rumi*, 125, v. 3; Forûzânfar (ed.), *Kulliyât-é shams yâ dîwân-é kabîr-e mawlânâ jalâluddîn Muhammad mashhûr ba-mawlawî*, v. 506; Gölpinarli, *Mevlânâ Celâleddin, Rubâîler*, D80, v. 109.

58. Can, *Hz. Mevlânâ'nin Rubâîleri*, v. 738; Ergin, *Rubâîlar of Rumi*, 128, v. 3; Forûzânfar (ed.), *Kulliyât-é shams yâ dîwân-é kabîr-e mawlânâ jalâluddîn Muhammad mashhûr ba-mawlawî*, v. 684; Gölpinarli, *Mevlânâ Celâleddin, Rubâîler*, D68, v. 6.

59. Can, *Hz. Mevlânâ'nin Rubâîleri*, v. 847; Ergin, *Rubâîlar of Rumi*, 131, v.1; Forûzânfar (ed.), *Kulliyât-é shams yâ dîwân-é kabîr-e mawlânâ jalâluddîn Muhammad mashhûr ba-mawlawî*, v. 795; Gölpinarli, *Mevlânâ Celâleddin, Rubâîler*, D76, v. 75.

60. Can, *Hz. Mevlânâ'nin Rubâîleri*, v. 820; Ergin, *Rubâîlar of Rumi*, 131, v. 4; Forûzânfar (ed.), *Kulliyât-é shams yâ dîwân-é kabîr-e mawlânâ jalâluddîn Muhammad mashhûr ba-mawlawî*, v. 767; Gölpinarli, *Mevlânâ Celâleddin, Rubâîler*, D76, v. 74.

61. Can, *Hz. Mevlânâ'nin Rubâîleri*, v. 743; Ergin, *Rubâîlar of Rumi*, 136, v. 3; Forûzânfar (ed.), *Kulliyât-é shams yâ dîwân-é kabîr-e mawlânâ jalâluddîn Muhammad mashhûr ba-mawlawî*, v. 689; Gölpinarli, *Mevlânâ Celâleddin, Rubâîler*, D67, v. 3.

62. Can, *Hz. Mevlânâ'nin Rubâîleri*, v. 548; Ergin, *Rubâîlar of Rumi*, 137, v. 4; Forûzânfar (ed.), *Kulliyât-é shams yâ dîwân-é kabîr-e mawlânâ jalâluddîn Muhammad mashhûr ba-mawlawî*, v. 493;

Gölpinarli, *Mevlânâ Celâleddin, Rubâîler,* D77, v. 88.

63. Can, *Hz. Mevlânâ'nin Rubâîleri,* v. 579; Ergin, *Rubâîlar of Rumi,* 139, v. 1; Forûzânfar (ed.), *Kulliyât-é shams yâ dîwân-é kabîr-e mawlânâ jalâluddîn Muhammad mashhûr ba-mawlawî,* v. 524; Gölpinarli, *Mevlânâ Celâleddin, Rubâîler,* D97, v. 264.

64. Can, *Hz. Mevlânâ'nin Rubâîleri,* v. 790; Ergin, *Rubâîlar of Rumi,* 143, v. 4; Forûzânfar (ed.), *Kulliyât-é shams yâ dîwân-é kabîr-e mawlânâ jalâluddîn Muhammad mashhûr ba-mawlawî,* v. 737; Gölpinarli, *Mevlânâ Celâleddin, Rubâîler,* D70, v. 24.

65. Can, *Hz. Mevlânâ'nin Rubâîleri,* v. 889; Ergin, *Rubâîlar of Rumi,* 146, v. 2; Forûzânfar (ed.), *Kulliyât-é shams yâ dîwân-é kabîr-e mawlânâ jalâluddîn Muhammad mashhûr ba-mawlawî,* v. 837; Gölpinarli, *Mevlânâ Celâleddin, Rubâîler,* D104, v. 319.

66. Can, *Hz. Mevlânâ'nin Rubâîleri,* v. 530; Ergin, *Rubâîlar of Rumi,* 147, v. 4; Forûzânfar (ed.), *Kulliyât-é shams yâ dîwân-é kabîr-e mawlânâ jalâluddîn Muhammad mashhûr ba-mawlawî,* v. 475; Gölpinarli, *Mevlânâ Celâleddin, Rubâîler,* D104-322.

67. Can, *Hz. Mevlânâ'nin Rubâîleri,* v. 844; Ergin, *Rubâîlar of Rumi,* 154, v. 2; Forûzânfar (ed.), *Kulliyât-é shams yâ dîwân-é kabîr-e mawlânâ jalâluddîn Muhammad mashhûr ba-mawlawî,* v. 792; Gölpinarli, *Mevlânâ Celâleddin, Rubâîler,* D105, v. 331.

68. Can, *Hz. Mevlânâ'nin Rubâîleri,* v. 708; Ergin, *Rubâîlar of Rumi,* 155, v. 1; Forûzânfar (ed.), *Kulliyât-é shams yâ dîwân-é kabîr-e mawlânâ jalâluddîn Muhammad mashhûr ba-mawlawî,* v. 654; Gölpinarli, *Mevlânâ Celâleddin, Rubâîler,* D70, v. 28.

69. Can, *Hz. Mevlânâ'nin Rubâîleri,* v. 634; Ergin, *Rubâîlar of Rumi,* 155, v. 2; Forûzânfar (ed.), *Kulliyât-é shams yâ dîwân-é kabîr-e mawlânâ jalâluddîn Muhammad mashhûr ba-mawlawî,* v. 579; Gölpinarli, *Mevlânâ Celâleddin, Rubâîler,* D82, v. 131.

70. Can, *Hz. Mevlânâ'nin Rubâîleri,* v. 857; Ergin, *Rubâîlar of Rumi,* 156, v. 3; Forûzânfar (ed.), *Kulliyât-é shams yâ dîwân-é kabîr-e mawlânâ jalâluddîn Muhammad mashhûr ba-mawlawî,* v. 805; Gölpinarli, *Mevlânâ Celâleddin, Rubâîler,* D83, v. 136.

71. Can, *Hz. Mevlânâ'nin Rubâîleri,* v. 878; Ergin, *Rubâîlar of Rumi,* 157, v. 1; Forûzânfar (ed.), *Kulliyât-é shams yâ dîwân-é kabîr-e mawlânâ jalâluddîn Muhammad mashhûr ba-mawlawî,* v. 826; Gölpinarli, *Mevlânâ Celâleddin, Rubâîler,* D106, v. 336.

72. Can, *Hz. Mevlânâ'nin Rubâîleri,* v.792; Ergin, *Rubâîlar of Rumi,* 159, v. 1; Forûzânfar (ed.), *Kulliyât-é shams yâ dîwân-é kabîr-e*

mawlânâ jalâluddîn Muhammad mashhûr ba-mawlawî, v. 739;
Gölpinarli, *Mevlânâ Celâleddin, Rubâîler*, D71, v. 30.

73. Can, *Hz. Mevlânâ'nin Rubâîleri*, v. 670; Ergin, *Rubâîlar of Rumi*,
159, v. 2; Forûzânfar (ed.), *Kulliyât-é shams yâ dîwân-é kabîr-e
mawlânâ jalâluddîn Muhammad mashhûr ba-mawlawî*, v. 616;
Gölpinarli, *Mevlânâ Celâleddin, Rubâîler*, D83, v. 139.

74. Can, *Hz. Mevlânâ'nin Rubâîleri*, v. 495; Ergin, *Rubâîlar of Rumi*,
159, v. 4; Forûzânfar (ed.), *Kulliyât-é shams yâ dîwân-é kabîr-e
mawlânâ jalâluddîn Muhammad mashhûr ba-mawlawî*, v. 440;
Gölpinarli, *Mevlânâ Celâleddin, Rubâîler*, D83, 142.

75. Can, *Hz. Mevlânâ'nin Rubâîleri*, v. 737; Ergin, *Rubâîlar of Rumi*,
160, v. 2; Forûzânfar (ed.), *Kulliyât-é shams yâ dîwân-é kabîr-e
mawlânâ jalâluddîn Muhammad mashhûr ba-mawlawî*, v. 683;
Gölpinarli, *Mevlânâ Celâleddin, Rubâîler*, D71, v. 31.

76. Can, *Hz. Mevlânâ'nin Rubâîleri*, v. 835; Ergin, *Rubâîlar of Rumi*,
160, v. 4; Forûzânfar (ed.), *Kulliyât-é shams yâ dîwân-é kabîr-e
mawlânâ jalâluddîn Muhammad mashhûr ba-mawlawî*, v. 783;
Gölpinarli, *Mevlânâ Celâleddin, Rubâîler*, D74, v. 68.

77. Can, *Hz. Mevlânâ'nin Rubâîleri*, v. 791; Ergin, *Rubâîlar of Rumi*,
161, v. 4; Forûzânfar (ed.), *Kulliyât-é shams yâ dîwân-é kabîr-e
mawlânâ jalâluddîn Muhammad mashhûr ba-mawlawî*, v. 738;
Gölpinarli, *Mevlânâ Celâleddin, Rubâîler*, D71, v. 32.

78. Can, *Hz. Mevlânâ'nin Rubâîleri*, v. 567; Ergin, *Rubâîlar of Rumi*,
163, v. 2; Forûzânfar (ed.), *Kulliyât-é shams yâ dîwân-é kabîr-e
mawlânâ jalâluddîn Muhammad mashhûr ba-mawlawî*, v. 512;
Gölpinarli, *Mevlânâ Celâleddin, Rubâîler*, D98, v. 269.

79. Can, *Hz. Mevlânâ'nin Rubâîleri*, v. 807; Ergin, *Rubâîlar of Rumi*,
198, v. 2; Forûzânfar (ed.), *Kulliyât-é shams yâ dîwân-é kabîr-e
mawlânâ jalâluddîn Muhammad mashhûr ba-mawlawî*, v. 754;
Gölpinarli, *Mevlânâ Celâleddin, Rubâîler*, D91, v. 210.

80. Can, *Hz. Mevlânâ'nin Rubâîleri*, v. 769; Ergin, *Rubâîlar of Rumi*,
165, v. 3; Forûzânfar (ed.), *Kulliyât-é shams yâ dîwân-é kabîr-e
mawlânâ jalâluddîn Muhammad mashhûr ba-mawlawî*, v. 715;
Gölpinarli, *Mevlânâ Celâleddin, Rubâîler*, D84, v. 149.

81. Can, *Hz. Mevlânâ'nin Rubâîleri*, v. 585; Ergin, *Rubâîlar of Rumi*,
168, v. 3; Forûzânfar (ed.), *Kulliyât-é shams yâ dîwân-é kabîr-e
mawlânâ jalâluddîn Muhammad mashhûr ba-mawlawî*, v. 530;
Gölpinarli, *Mevlânâ Celâleddin, Rubâîler*, D107, v. 350.

82. Can, *Hz. Mevlânâ'nin Rubâîleri*, v. 583; Ergin, *Rubâîlar of Rumi*, 169, v. 2; Forûzânfar (ed.), *Kulliyât-é shams yâ dîwân-é kabîr-e mawlânâ jalâluddîn Muhammad mashhûr ba-mawlawî*, v. 528; Gölpinarli, *Mevlânâ Celâleddin, Rubâîler*, D71, v. 34.

83. Can, *Hz. Mevlânâ'nin Rubâîleri*, v. 646; Ergin, *Rubâîlar of Rumi*, 170, v. 1; Forûzânfar (ed.), *Kulliyât-é shams yâ dîwân-é kabîr-e mawlânâ jalâluddîn Muhammad mashhûr ba-mawlawî*, v. 592; Gölpinarli, *Mevlânâ Celâleddin, Rubâîler*, D85, v. 157.

84. Can, *Hz. Mevlânâ'nin Rubâîleri*, v. 624; Ergin, *Rubâîlar of Rumi*, 170, v. 2; Forûzânfar (ed.), *Kulliyât-é shams yâ dîwân-é kabîr-e mawlânâ jalâluddîn Muhammad mashhûr ba-mawlawî*, v. 569; Gölpinarli, *Mevlânâ Celâleddin, Rubâîler*, D85, v. 159.

85. Can, *Hz. Mevlânâ'nin Rubâîleri*, v. 528; Ergin, *Rubâîlar of Rumi*, 171, v. 3; Forûzânfar (ed.), *Kulliyât-é shams yâ dîwân-é kabîr-e mawlânâ jalâluddîn Muhammad mashhûr ba-mawlawî*, v. 473; Gölpinarli, *Mevlânâ Celâleddin, Rubâîler*, D85, v. 156.

86. Can, *Hz. Mevlânâ'nin Rubâîleri*, v. 853; Ergin, *Rubâîlar of Rumi*, 172, v. 2; Forûzânfar (ed.), *Kulliyât-é shams yâ dîwân-é kabîr-e mawlânâ jalâluddîn Muhammad mashhûr ba-mawlawî*, v. 801; Gölpinarli, *Mevlânâ Celâleddin, Rubâîler*, D109, v. 359.

87. Can, *Hz. Mevlânâ'nin Rubâîleri*, v. 647; Ergin, *Rubâîlar of Rumi*, 176, v. 4; Forûzânfar (ed.), *Kulliyât-é shams yâ dîwân-é kabîr-e mawlânâ jalâluddîn Muhammad mashhûr ba-mawlawî*, v. 593; Gölpinarli, *Mevlânâ Celâleddin, Rubâîler*, D86, 169.

88. Can, *Hz. Mevlânâ'nin Rubâîleri*, v. 759; Ergin, *Rubâîlar of Rumi*, 177, v. 1; Forûzânfar (ed.), *Kulliyât-é shams yâ dîwân-é kabîr-e mawlânâ jalâluddîn Muhammad mashhûr ba-mawlawî*, v. 705; Gölpinarli, *Mevlânâ Celâleddin, Rubâîler*, D109, v. 364.

89. Can, *Hz. Mevlânâ'nin Rubâîleri*, v. 784; Ergin, *Rubâîlar of Rumi*, 177, v. 3; Forûzânfar (ed.), *Kulliyât-é shams yâ dîwân-é kabîr-e mawlânâ jalâluddîn Muhammad mashhûr ba-mawlawî*, v. 731; Gölpinarli, *Mevlânâ Celâleddin, Rubâîler*, D71, v. 36.

90. Can, *Hz. Mevlânâ'nin Rubâîleri*, v. 597; Ergin, *Rubâîlar of Rumi*, 178, v. 2; Forûzânfar (ed.), *Kulliyât-é shams yâ dîwân-é kabîr-e mawlânâ jalâluddîn Muhammad mashhûr ba-mawlawî*, v. 542; Gölpinarli, *Mevlânâ Celâleddin, Rubâîler*, D110, v. 368.

91. Can, *Hz. Mevlânâ'nin Rubâîleri*, v. 886; Ergin, *Rubâîlar of Rumi*, 179, v. 4; Forûzâfar (ed.), *Kulliyâ-é shams yâ dîwân-é kabîr-e*

mawlânâ jalâluddîn Muhammad mashhûr ba-mawlawî, v. 834; Gölpinarli, *Mevlânâ Celâleddin, Rubâîler,* D86, v. 164.

92. Can, *Hz. Mevlânâ'nin Rubâîleri,* v. 955; Ergin, *Rubâîlar of Rumi,* 180, v. 1; Gölpinarli, *Mevlânâ Celâleddin, Rubâîler,* D109, v. 363.

93. Can, *Hz. Mevlânâ'nin Rubâîleri,* v. 2121; Ergin, *Rubâîlar of Rumi,* 442, v. 2; Forûzânfar (ed.), *Kulliyât-é shams yâ dîwân-é kabîr-e mawlânâ jalâluddîn Muhammad mashhûr ba-mawlawî,* v. 1929; Gölpinarli, *Mevlânâ Celâleddin, Rubâîler,* Y207, v. 85.

94. Can, *Hz. Mevlânâ'nin Rubâîleri,* v. 547; Ergin, *Rubâîlar of Rumi,* 185, v. 4; Forûzânfar (ed.), *Kulliyât-é shams yâ dîwân-é kabîr-e mawlânâ jalâluddîn Muhammad mashhûr ba-mawlawî,* v. 492; Gölpinarli, *Mevlânâ Celâleddin, Rubâîler,* D88, v. 184.

95. Can, *Hz. Mevlânâ'nin Rubâîleri,* v. 687; Ergin, *Rubâîlar of Rumi,* 186, v. 2; Forûzânfar (ed.), *Kulliyât-é shams yâ dîwân-é kabîr-e mawlânâ jalâluddîn Muhammad mashhûr ba-mawlawî,* v. 633; Gölpinarli, *Mevlânâ Celâleddin, Rubâîler,* D88, v. 183.

96. Can, *Hz. Mevlânâ'nin Rubâîleri,* v. 770; Ergin, *Rubâîlar of Rumi,* 187, v. 1; Forûzânfar (ed.), *Kulliyât-é shams yâ dîwân-é kabîr-e mawlânâ jalâluddîn Muhammad mashhûr ba-mawlawî,* v. 716; Gölpinarli, *Mevlânâ Celâleddin, Rubâîler,* D111, v. 378.

97. Can, *Hz. Mevlânâ'nin Rubâîleri,* v. 798; Ergin, *Rubâîlar of Rumi,* 189, v. 3; Forûzânfar (ed.), *Kulliyât-é shams yâ dîwân-é kabîr-e mawlânâ jalâluddîn Muhammad mashhûr ba-mawlawî,* v. 745; Gölpinarli, *Mevlânâ Celâleddin, Rubâîler,* D72, v. 43.

98. Can, *Hz. Mevlânâ'nin Rubâîleri,* v. 84; Ergin, *Rubâîlar of Rumi,* 31, v. 3; Forûzânfar (ed.), *Kulliyât-é shams yâ dîwân-é kabîr-e mawlânâ jalâluddîn Muhammad mashhûr ba-mawlawî,* v. 71; Gölpinarli, *Mevlânâ Celâleddin, Rubâîler,* B27, v. 28.

99. Ergin, *Rubâîlar of Rumi,* 200, v.1; Gölpinarli, *Mevlânâ Celâleddin, Rubâîler,* D91, v. 207.

100.Can, *Hz. Mevlânâ'nin Rubâîleri,* v. 705; Ergin, *Rubâîlar of Rumi,* 164, v. 2; Forûzânfar (ed.), *Kulliyât-é shams yâ dîwân-é kabîr-e mawlânâ jalâluddîn Muhammad mashhûr ba-mawlawî,* v. 651; Gölpinarli, *Mevlânâ Celâleddin, Rubâîler,* D98, v. 270.

Bibliography

Can, Şefik. *Hz. Mevlânâ'nin Rubâîleri.* Ankara, Turkey: T.C. Kûltûr Bakanliği Yayinlari/2752 Yayimlar Dairesi /Başkanliği / Sanat-Ebediyat Eserleri Dizise/3655-120, 2001.

Ergin, Nevit. *Dîvân-i Kabîr Meter 9.* Los Angeles: Echo Publications, 1996.

----------. *Rubâîlar of Rumi.* Los Angeles: Echo Publications, 2015.

Forûzânfar Badî'uzzamân, ed. *Kulliyât-é shams yâ dîwân-é kabîr-e mawlânâ jalâluddîn Muhammad mashhûr ba-mawlawî.* Tehrân, Iran: University of Tehrân, 1957-1967.

Gölpinarli, Abdulbaki. *Mevlânâ Celâleddin, Rubâîler.* Ankara, Turkey: Ajans-Türk Matbaacilik Sanayi, 1982.

About the Author

Nevit O. Ergin devoted his life to the same spiritual path as Mevlana Jalaluddin Rumi. He is the only person to have translated into English Rumi's entire *Dîvân-i Kebîr*—44,000 verses in 22 volumes. He also translated all 2,217 of Rumi's rubais. His translations are not just intellectual, but truly inspired. He spent over 60 years of his life "trying to get rid of this earth before it gets rid of me." He died in July 2015.

www.ingramcontent.com/pod-product-compliance
Lightning Source LLC
LaVergne TN
LVHW051507080426
835509LV00017B/1951